Around The Year Quilt Book

Twelve beautiful Rosie & Bear blocks.
One wonderful heirloom quilt.

HELEN DICKSON

Bustle & Sew
www.bustleandsew.com

For my daughter Rosie, a little girl so long ago and far away, who still loves to set off on adventures! And for my husband who has given me so much encouragement and support.

A Bustle & Sew Book

Copyright © Bustle & Sew Limited 2012

The right of Helen Dickson to be identified as the author of this work has been asserted in accordance with the Copyright, Designs and Patents Act 1988.

All rights reserved. No part of this publication may be reproduced, stored in a retrieval system or transmitted in any form, or by any means, without the prior written permission of the author, nor be otherwise circulated in any form of binding or cover other than that in which it is published and without a similar condition being imposed on the subsequent purchaser.

Every effort has been made to ensure that all the information in this book is accurate. However, due to differing conditions, tools and individual skills, the publisher cannot be responsible for any injuries, losses and other damages that may result from the use of the information in this book.

First published 2012 by:
Bustle & Sew
Coombe Leigh
Chillington
Kingsbridge
Devon TQ7 2LE
UK

www.bustleandsew.com
ISBN: 978-0-9570093-1-8

CONTENTS

The Story Begins ….	Page 5
Using this Book	Page 7
Tools and Materials	Page 9
Transferring your Designs	Page 13
Material Requirements	Page 15
How to Embroider Fur	Page 17
Around the Year Quilt Blocks	Page 21
January	Page 22
February	Page 27
March	Page 32
April	Page 37
May	Page 42
June	Page 47
July	Page 52
August	Page 57
September	Page 62
October	Page 67
November	Page 72
December	Page 77
Testing your Seam Allowances	Page 82
Piecing your Quilt Top	Page 84
Finishing your Quilt	Page 88
Adding your Label	Page 89
Glossary of Embroidery Stitches	Page 90

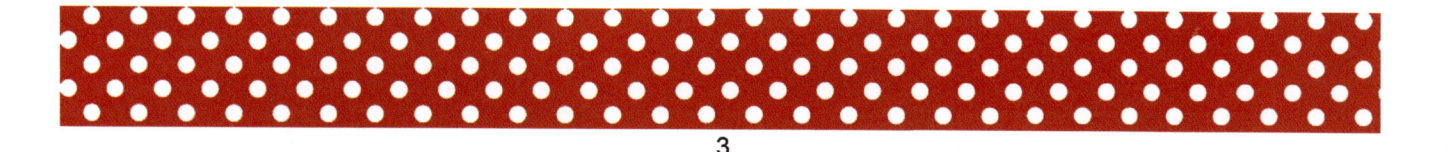

Helen Dickson started her online pattern business, Bustle & Sew, in 2009.

She creates designs for patterns that are lively, interesting and fresh, and that she hopes will inspire others to pick up fabric and thread to produce their own piece of work with all the sense of achievement that brings.

She loves stitching and is passionate about sharing with others through her blog and e-zine.

Connect with Helen through her blog:

www.bustleandsew.com/blog

Discover her patterns on her website:

www.bustleandsew.com

If you like Helen's patterns, then why not consider the Bustle & Sew e-zine, an eclectic mixture of her original designs, vintage stitching, features, articles and even a recipe page contributed by her now grown-up daughter Rosie? It's the nicest, best value way to build your library of Bustle & Sew designs. Learn more here:

www.bustleandsew.com/magazine

THE STORY BEGINS …

The idea for my Rosie & Bear Calendar Quilt came to me as I was looking through my collection of photograph albums from those long-ago, far-away days when I had a very small daughter called Rosie …

My albums contained photos of Rosie enjoying summer holidays, Christmas celebrations, picnics on the beach and parties in the garden. Even when he couldn't be spotted in the pictures, you could be sure that her faithful companion, Bear, was not too far away. Indeed, he was probably just out of camera range, getting into some mischief or other while nobody was taking any notice of him.

Although Rosie is all grown-up now, she still treasures Bear, who has become quite an elderly gentleman. These days he is content to wait quietly on the end of her bed, snoozing away the hours until Rosie returns home in the evenings to tell him all about her days. He is such a very good listener, and <u>never</u> reveals the secrets he learns.

I have always loved vintage blocks of the month, featuring all kinds of animals or flowers through the seasons of the year, so popular in the mid-20th century. Although I have discovered lots of lovely contemporary embroidery designs, when I started searching for calendar blocks to make into a quilt, I couldn't find any that really appealed to me. That was when I decided to create my own "Rosie and Bear" series.

I like to keep things simple when I'm designing and so, whether you're a quilter who is trying out freestyle embroidery, or a stitcher who wants to create a special quilt, you're sure to achieve a good result.

There's nothing complicated at all about this project. In fact, the only problem I had along the way was deciding what to put in and what to leave out of the set of quilt blocks. That's why you'll find some additional Rosie and Bear designs on my Bustle & Sew website if you'd like to stitch some extra Rosie and Bear pictures.

And of course if you have a special child of your own in your life, then why not consider customising Rosie, perhaps changing her hair, or skin colour to reflect your own child's? This is sure to make your quilt very special to, and treasured by, its lucky recipient.

I hope you have as much fun making your very own quilt as I had putting this book together for you.

Helen Dickson
June 2012

USING THIS BOOK ...

You will find all the material requirements for making the whole quilt on page 15, before the individual patterns for each block of the month.

I am sure that some readers might be planning to make individual blocks - maybe stitching a single design for a particular project, or perhaps making their quilts over an extended period of time. To make it easier for those who intend to do this, I have also given the material requirements for each individual block at the beginning of its section.

As different stitchers prefer different methods of transferring the design to the fabric, I have provided the embroidery patterns both the right way round and reversed to suit your preferred method of transfer. I have also included guidance on how to transfer your design.

As well as a glossary of perhaps the less familiar stitches at the back of this book, I have also included guidance for embroidering fur. Whether you're a newbie stitcher or more experienced, I recommend you read this before starting to stitch as you will find lots of hints and tips to help you make Bear's fur the best it can be. Lots of stitchers are put off by the idea of embroidering fur, but it really isn't that hard at all.

Bear is the only solid part of the embroidery - this is because he's the only character that remains unchanged to the present day. Childhood is very fleeting and the little Rosie in those blocks simply doesn't exist any more. Now my daughter is a lovely young woman, and I'm very proud of her, but she is quite different to the child of 20 years ago of course!

I think you'll discover that both the embroidery and piecing the quilt top are suprisingly easy, and very enjoyable to do.

And finally ... don't forget to label your quilt on the back when you've finished. I've included a Rosie & Bear label for you to use for this purpose. Future generations will thank you for taking the time and trouble to do this as "Granny's Quilt" is sure to be loved by your children and your children's children too!

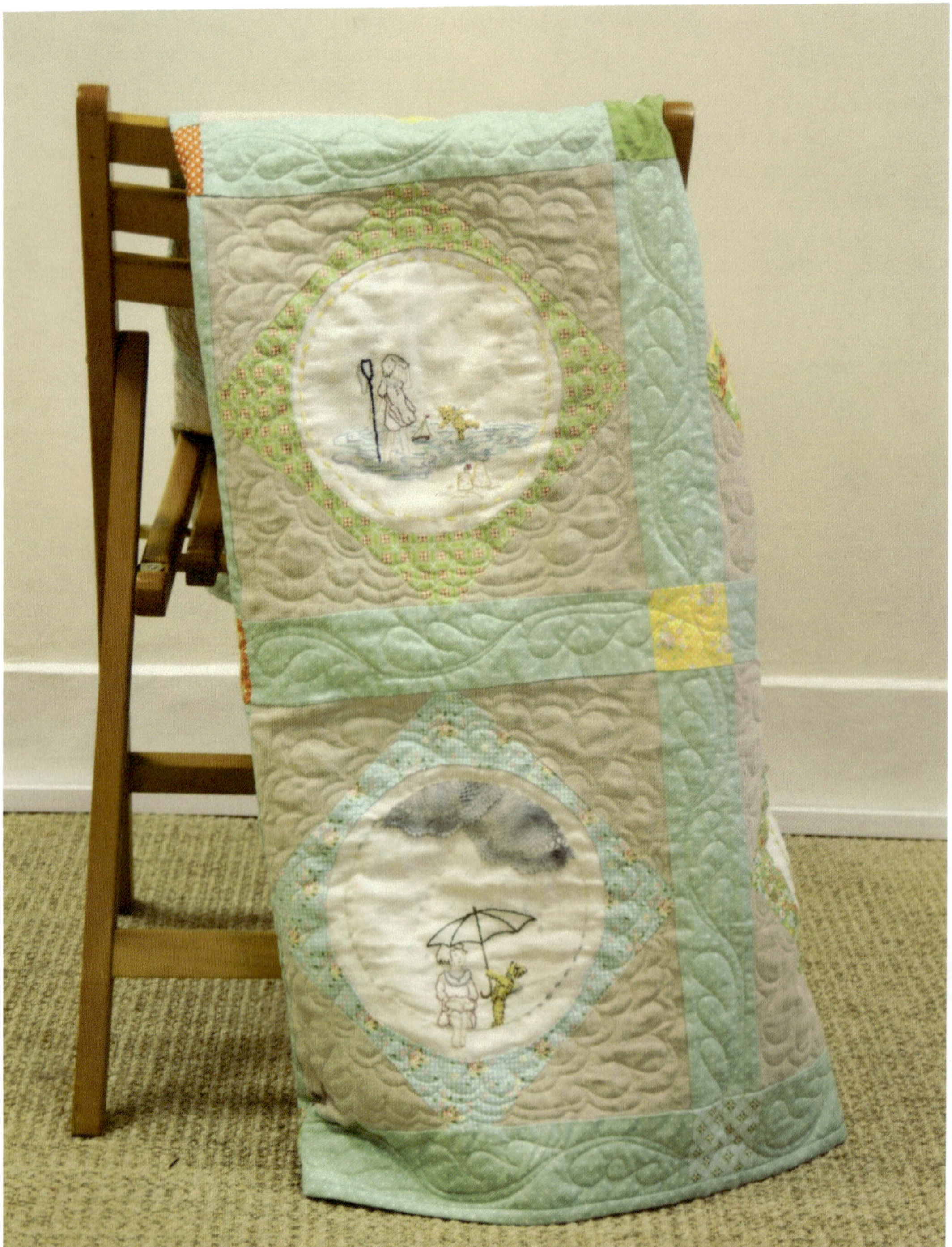

TOOLS AND MATERIALS

One of the great things about a project like this is that you don't need to purchase lots of expensive tools and materials to get you started. But don't economise on the items you do purchase - you'll be investing a lots of time and energy in your Calendar Quilt, so purchase items that you'll enjoy using and that will give you good results.

You will need the following basic items:

FOR THE EMBROIDERY

NEEDLES

Did you know that the steel needles we use today were introduced in the 16th century? And since then needles have been developed for all kinds of techniques. Embroidery needles have sharp points and long eyes to make it easier to thread multiple lengths of floss. It's advisable to change your needle regularly as they can become blunt or even bent which will affect the quality of your work.

Choose a good brand of needle - cheaper brands may be roughly finished and any rough bits will snag on your floss or fabric. They may also bend or break more easily. For embroidery the needles of choice are "Sharps". The stitching in this quilt uses 1 or 2 strands of floss, and for this I would recommend a number 6 needle.

EMBROIDERY FLOSS

Floss is available in a huge variety of colours. I have specified DMC floss in this book as it is both good quality and widely available. You can of course substitute colours, but do please be aware that you are unlikely to find an exact match for the specified colour which will affect the look of your quilt.

Do not be tempted to economise by purchasing cheap floss as this is likely to tangle and break, will not give such a good finish and, in the worst case, may not be colourfast on washing.

I like to store my floss on bobbins as using them direct from the skein results (for me at least!) in a tangled mess. Also, you can label the bobbins with the floss colour number, whilst the paper bands on the skeins are likely to slip off and become lost, so you won't have any idea which is which.

Stranded cotton floss comes in six strands - most of the blocks in this quilt use just two strands in your needle at any one time. Cut a length of floss before splitting into strands - and don't make the length too long (the distance from your wrist to your elbow is generally accepted to be about right) or it is likely to become tangled.

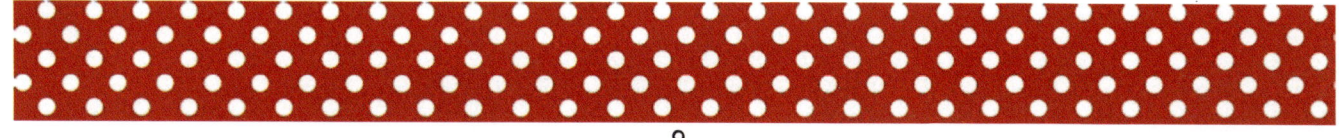

EMBROIDERY HOOP

Choosing the right frame or hoop is quite a personal decision. Indeed, many stitchers prefer to work without one at all. I much prefer to use a hoop as it keeps my background fabric stretched and stable so I can maintain an even tension as I stitch. Working without a hoop may lead to uneven stitches, wrinkled fabric and a generally poor finish.

Hoops consist simply of two circles placed one inside the other, trapping the material between them. The outer hoop is then tightened by turning a screw at the side.

Hoops can be made of wood or plastic in different sizes and some can be attached to a table clamp or stand. The projects in this book were worked in a 9" hoop - large enough to show the majority of the design without moving the hoop around too much, but also small enough to be easy to hold in the hand to work with.

To stop your fabric slipping, bind the inner hoop with fabric strips, cotton tape or bias binding and secure the ends with stitches. If the fabric you've chosen is easily marked or damaged, then you may wish to bind the outer hoop as well.

To "hoop up" your fabric, lay the inner hoop on a clean flat surface and place your fabric right side up over it. Using the screw on the outer hoop, adjust it so the outer hoop fits snugly over both the inner hoop and the fabric. Push the outer hoop down, gently pulling the fabric taut. Tighten the screw.

COPY OF YOUR STITCHING GUIDE

I would recommend that you print off the stitching guide for the block you're working on and keep it close to hand. This way it will be easily available for referring to, making notes on, and mopping up any stray coffee spills with!

WORK BAG OR BOX

To keep your work nice and clean and fresh it's important to store it safely.

If you don't have a workbox, then even an old pillowcase is sufficient to protect your stitching from dust, dirt, kids and pets! And one of those plastic storage boxes with lots of little compartments to stop the contents rattling around is ideal to store all your stitching stuff.

FOR ASSEMBLY AND QUILTING

For piecing and quilting your finished top use only good quality 100% cotton or cotton/polyester thread. Don't be tempted by those cheap cones of thread you can sometimes find in the bargain bin at sewing shops. You'll end up with tangled or broken thread, and find getting a good line of stitching on your machine is almost impossible.

Choose a neutral coloured thread for the piecing and quilting and use the same coloured thread in both the needle and bobbin if you are quilting the finished piece yourself.

Whether you have your quilt professionally long-arm quilted, or do it yourself, and depending upon your batting, you may need to hand-quilt the embroidered Blocks. Do this in a colour to match the background fabric as you want this quilting to disappear.

QUILTING NEEDLES

Although the majority of the quilt is finished by machine, you will probably need to quilt the calendar blocks themselves by hand unless your batting allows for quilting lines more than 8" apart.

The blocks are quilted by hand to avoid damaging the embroidery and also so that the stitches are small, unobtrusive and sensitive to the design. Quilting the embroidered blocks will prevent them from "bagging" in use.

Quilting needles are short, with a small rounded eye and are good for making small stitches on heavy or multiple layers of fabric.

MACHINE NEEDLES

For piecing your shapes together choose medium sized machine needles (70/10 or 80/12). Universal needles are fine for quilting weight cotton fabrics. If you are planning to quilt the project yourself, then for the quilting choose heavier (90/14) machine quilting needles. If your needles break often during quilting, then you may need to change to a heavier needle.

Remember that needles become blunt very quickly, so change them after about 10 - 12 hours of sewing. If you stitch with a blunt needle this will adversely affect the quality of your sewing.

ROTARY CUTTER

Choose a 45 mm or 60 mm cutter - one that will fit comfortably into your hand. Be sure to use a sharp blade - normally a cutter blade will last for two to three projects before it needs replacing. Also be sure to retract the blade into the safety cover every time you put it down - those blades are SHARP!!

CUTTING MAT

You'll need a reasonably sized self-healing cutting mat - at least 18" x 24" and larger if possible. Make sure the grid lines are easy to read. The larger your mat, the less frequently you'll need to move your fabric while you're cutting it, so a larger mat both saves time and makes your cutting more accurate.

QUILTING RULER

There is a bewildering variety of shapes and sizes of clear plastic quilting rulers available. For this project you'll need a 6" x 24" rectangle shape.

SAFETY PINS

Those designed for quilters have a slightly curved shape. If you're using pins to baste your quilt then you'll need at least 100 and possibly more.

I personally like to use a basting gun. I know opinion is divided on this method, but you might like to try it.

A basting gun inserts tiny plastic tags through the layers of fabric and batting to hold them securely in place. It's really quick and easy once you get the hang of it and the tags are very inexpensive to purchase.

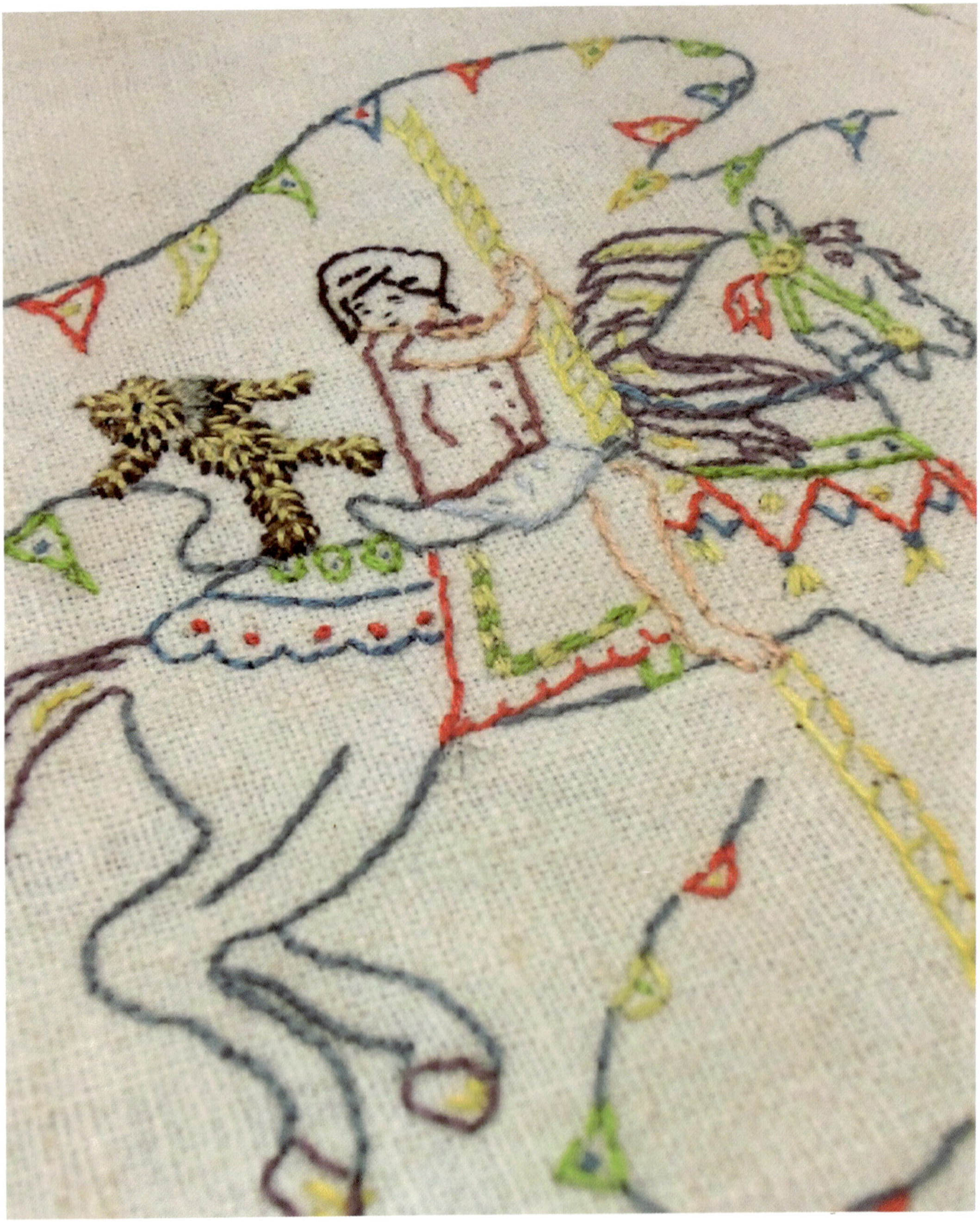

TRANSFERRING THE DESIGNS

Before you can begin to stitch your first block, you'll need to transfer the design to your fabric. I have included all the designs at their actual size so you don't need to spend time re-sizing them. You'll also see that I've reproduced them in both original and reverse versions. This is because there are various ways of transferring your design to your fabric and the method you select will affect which way round you need the original printed design to be.

TRACING THE DESIGN

This works well onto plain, light-coloured fabric, so is perhaps the best method to use for these blocks. You can use either a water soluble or a permanent marker with a fine tip.

Print the design outline and tape it onto a light box or window (a bright sunny day is best for this). You can even display the design at the size you want on your computer screen and max the brightness. If you don't have a lightbox you can make your own using any empty plastic storage box and a light bulb (but don't leave it unattended when it's switched on).

Now tape your fabric over the tracing, ensuring that it's square (ie the grain is aligned horizontally and vertically). Trace the design onto the fabric with your marker. Use a smooth continuous line for best results.

Note: Air or light fade pens are not suitable as the design will fade and vanish over time, especially in strong light.

DRESSMAKER'S CARBON TRANSFER PAPER

This comes in small packages containing about five different colours of carbon. Place your fabric right side up on a clean, smooth, hard surface (you may wish to tape it down to stop it slipping).

Tape your carbon onto the fabric and your printed design on top of that. Using a sharp pencil, stylus or ballpoint pen and a firm steady stroke, carefully trace over the lines of your design in long continuous lines.

Be very careful not to puncture the paper as this will leave a nasty blob on your fabric. As the transfer paper is available in many colours, just choose the one that shows best on your fabric.

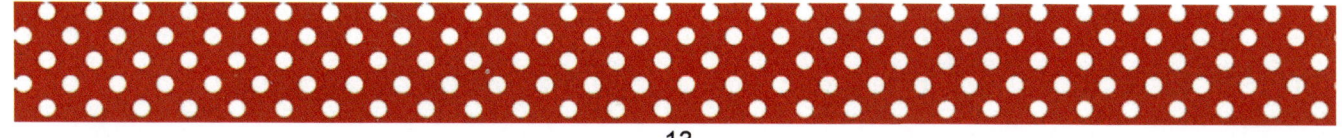

TRANSFER PENS AND PENCILS

For this technique you'll need the mirrored design. Transfer pens and pencils are very easy to use - just follow the instructions that come with them.

You trace the printed pattern with your pen or pencil, then turn the paper face down onto the right side of your fabric (again you might like to tape both paper and fabric to avoid slipping). Then you iron your tracing onto the fabric. The ink or pencil marks will be transferred to the fabric in the same way as a commercially produced iron-on pattern.

BUBBLEJET PRINTING

You can use your bubblejet printer to print directly on to the fabric using freezer paper as backing or purchase specially prepared fabric.

Please refer to the manufacturer's guidelines if you plan to use this technique.

Whichever technique you use, ensure that your design is centred on your fabric square.

MATERIAL REQUIREMENTS

The finished quilt measures 46" x 62" and will sit comfortably on a single bed.

To make the complete quilt you will need:

FABRIC

- 12 x 12" squares of cream linen or linen/cotton blend for the embroidered blocks
- 12 x 10" squares of floral fabric. I used the squares from a Moda Layer Cake - these are the perfect size. The collection I used is "Flora" by Lauren and Jessi Jung for Moda.
- 20 x 3 ½" squares floral fabric in colours to compliment your larger squares (cut from the same layer cake if you're using one)
- 1 ½ yards of 44" wide biscuit coloured fabric for triangles to frame floral squares.
- 3 yards mini-polka-dot fabric for sashing and binding your quilt

FLOSS

DMC stranded cotton floss in shade numbers:

67, 111, 162, 166, 257, 277, 310, 315, 321, 347, 386, 434, 504, 518, 581, 676, 680, 704, 720, 729, 740, 742, 754, 758, 761, 775, 815, 838, 839, 862, 904, 906, 907, 935, 938, 973, 977, 3021, 3031, 3041, 3325, 3831, 3841, 3862, 3864, 4030, 4050, 4065, 4070, 4075, 4080, 4100, 4126, 4180, 4190, L833, Blanc and Ecru.

NOTIONS

- Cream thread for your sewing machine - needle and bobbin.
- Temporary fabric adhesive spray
- 8" and 8 ¼" diameter circle templates (cut from card is fine)
- Temporary fabric marker pen

Note: Fabric for embroidery must be non-stretchy.

If you're using pre-cut fabrics such as the layer cake that I used for my 12 inner blocks, then pre-washing is not recommended. But if you're cutting your own fabric, then depending upon the quality and maker, pre-washing can be a good idea. It will prevent any uneven shrinkage spoiling your finished quilt.

October

August

January

April

16

HOW TO EMBROIDER FUR

The quilt blocks in this book feature my daughter, Rosie, and her childhood friend Bear. Although Rosie is very simple to embroider, using stem and back stitch, Bear is shown in all his furry glory. I know the thought of stitching fur can be a bit scary if you've never tried it before. But don't worry - it's really quite easy - and with Bear's help I'm going to show you how…

You might like to practise your fur embroidery before starting your quilt, in which case you will need a 6" square piece of cotton or linen fabric suitable for embroidery. You will also need stranded cotton embroidery floss in dark chocolate, milk chocolate, toffee and fudge colours *(OK that's very dark brown, mid to dark brown, light brown and golden yellow colours. But as I recall that Bear was always very fond of sweets I thought I'd use our common language!)* You'll also need some black for his eye and the tiniest little bit of white to put the sparkle in his eye. Using linen floss in with the cotton gives interest to the texture as the linen is matt which contrasts nicely with the shine of the cotton. But if you can't get linen floss, then it's fine to use all cotton.

First transfer your Bear onto your fabric. My Bear measures between 2 ½" and 3" tall - small enough so that there's not too much stitching but large enough to be able to delineate the different shades of fur clearly and effectively.

IMPORTANT: You will be using 2 strands of floss throughout unless specified otherwise.

Hoop up and take a good look at the soon-to-be furry fellow. If you have a pet, then take a good look at him or her too - or check out some animal pictures.

Notice the direction in which the fur grows. ALWAYS away from the nose

The nose, therefore, is the focus of all your fur stitches. And look at how their fur overlaps so that the fur nearest the nose lies on top of fur further down the body.

This is the first key to achieving realistic Bear fur - getting the *direction* of your stitching correct.

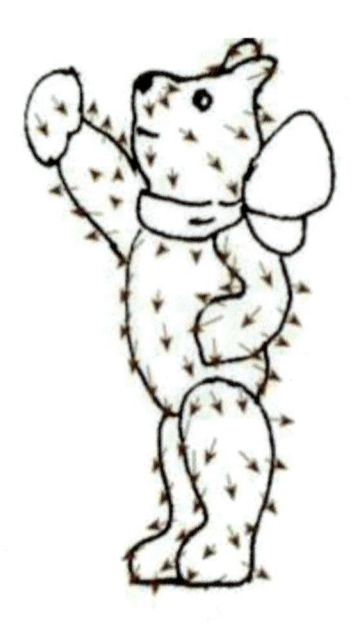

Here's Bear, looking a bit like a pin cushion. The arrows show the direction of his fur and you can see that they're all directed away from his nose. Imagine smoothing him .. you never smooth your dog, cat or rabbit from tail to nose as that would ruffle their fur the wrong way - always from nose to tail.

The second important thing to consider before you even thread your needle is shading. Here's a little bear I drew a few years ago:

Because I'm not a very good artist you'll be able to see some pencil lines around the edge of the bear. But the positions of his arms, legs and face are totally shown through shading. You can see that his fur is dark where there are shadows, or his limb is further away, and brighter where his body catches the light, eg on his round bottom or the backs of his arms.

This is the effect you're aiming to achieve with your needle and floss. You'll work darker stitches where the fur would be in shadow and, blending as you go, work towards lighter stitches where there are highlights, eg on his nice fat tummy. This sounds more difficult than it is, it's really much easier to show you than to try to explain in writing.

So, thread your needle with two strands of milk chocolate (medium brown) floss. You will start at the bottom of the bear as this will ensure that your later stitches will overlap your earlier ones correctly.

Abandon any thought of stitching along the outline. Bear is fluffy, not hard or smooth and outline is for crisp, solid edges. Work your stitches at an angle to his limbs, as though his fur was falling softly:

So far so good. Keep your transfer close to you as it's easy to lose track of the shape you're trying to achieve. If you find it easier then work Bear in separate parts - one limb at a time, then his tummy and finally his head.

Now you've worked the shadows. Notice how the back leg is darker than the front, there is a line of dark fur along the back of his arm and front leg, also below his ribbon and at the back of his head.

Use your toffee-coloured floss to fill in the gaps between the chocolate floss and also scatter a few stitches in the areas you're going to highlight - even highlights have shadows and fur is never just one colour - check out that pet again!

Before you add more stitches to his head you might find it's easier to indicate where his eye will be with black floss and his nose with very dark brown.

This means you can work right up to them with confidence. I usually work his ribbon at this stage too - he's really starting to look like Bear!

Don't worry if you can't easily see the boundaries between his limbs, eg where his arm comes over his tummy. We have a secret weapon to deal with that. Just keep stitching and shading. Remember to keep your stitches irregular - no straight lines please!

Finish the toffee coloured stitching on his head, again remembering your shading. Pay particular attention to the paw holding the flower - the actual paw will be lighter than the arm behind it as it's further forward in space.

Now thread your fudge-coloured floss and fill in all the gaps between the stitches. Try to work as thickly as possible to make his fur look lush, but if there are spaces, then don't worry too much.

But there's still something missing - the sparkle in Bear's eye and a little extra depth of shadow along his arm and other areas.

Thread your needle with ONE strand of very dark brown floss.

Work small stitches along the inner edge of Bear's forward arm, the boundary between his back legs, the deepest shadow around his ribbon and where his paw is bent forward to hold his flower.

Look how those hard-to-see stitches have made all the difference. Now you can clearly see Bear's arm, legs and other deeply shaded areas.

Finally with one strand of white, add a little sparkle to his eye, and if liked, a little pink for the insides of his ears.

THE QUILT BLOCKS

*"January brings the snow,
Makes our feet and fingers glow."*

JANUARY SNOWBALL FIGHT

There are 31 days in January, which was named in the ancient Roman calendar after Janus, the god of beginnings and endings. Janus was represented as a two-faced god, looking backward and forward at the same time - to the old year and the new.

Here in England, January has always been regarded as the coldest month and, although the days are growing longer, they will become colder before spring arrives. Snow and ice are very likely in January - and here the naughty pair are making the most of a heavy snowfall. Rosie has built a beautiful snowman and Bear is perched on top, with a huge pawful of snow ready to fling at Rosie.

MATERIAL REQUIREMENTS

FOR THE EMBROIDERY

12" square cream linen or linen/cotton blend

DMC floss in colours 67, 162, 257, 310, 386, 676, 720, 742, 775, 825, 3726, 3862, 3864, 4065, L833 blanc

STITCHES USED

Chain stitch, stem stitch, straight stitch, satin stitch, French knots, running stitch, back stitch.

Please see the Stitch Glossary at the back of this book if you are unfamiliar with working any of these stitches.

NOTES ON WORKING

For detailed instructions on working Bear's fur, please see the section "How to Embroider Fur" on page 17 of this book.

The design is worked in two strands of floss throughout unless otherwise stated.

Bear's ribbon is stitched in 4065 satin stitch. Change the direction of your satin stitch to delineate the knot and loops of his bow.

Rosie's features are worked in a single strand of dark brown.

Frame the design with running stitch using all 6 strands of 4065. You will probably need a larger needle to do this.

TIP OF THE MONTH

The first thing to consider when getting ready to thread your needle is the size of your thread and your choice of needle. They should complement each other.

You don't want to use a needle that's too LARGE for your thread, as it will leave visible holes in your fabric. On the other hand, you don't want to use a needle that's too SMALL for your thread, either – you'll cause yourself a lot of difficulty when stitching, having to tug really hard to get the needle and thread through the fabric (which could well break either needle or thread)

After doing a bit of needlework, you'll probably get the hang of what's right and what's not for your needle and thread. An easy rule of thumb is that the thickness of your needle should match the thickness of the thread.

Sun 742 chain stitch

Trees 257 back stitch
Snow 162 stem stitch

Rosie:

Coat 3726 back & stem stitch

Scarf 257 back and stem stitch

Wellies 815 back stitch

Hair 3862 back stitch
Skin 386 back stitch

Snowballs 67, 775, blanc French knots (mix colours)

Bristles mix 3862, L833 & 310 straight stitch

Hat 257 stem stitch

Broomstick L833 Chain stitch

Snowman 67 stem stitch

Eyes, mouth and buttons 310 French knots

Carrot for nose 720 satin stitch

Snow 67 stem stitch

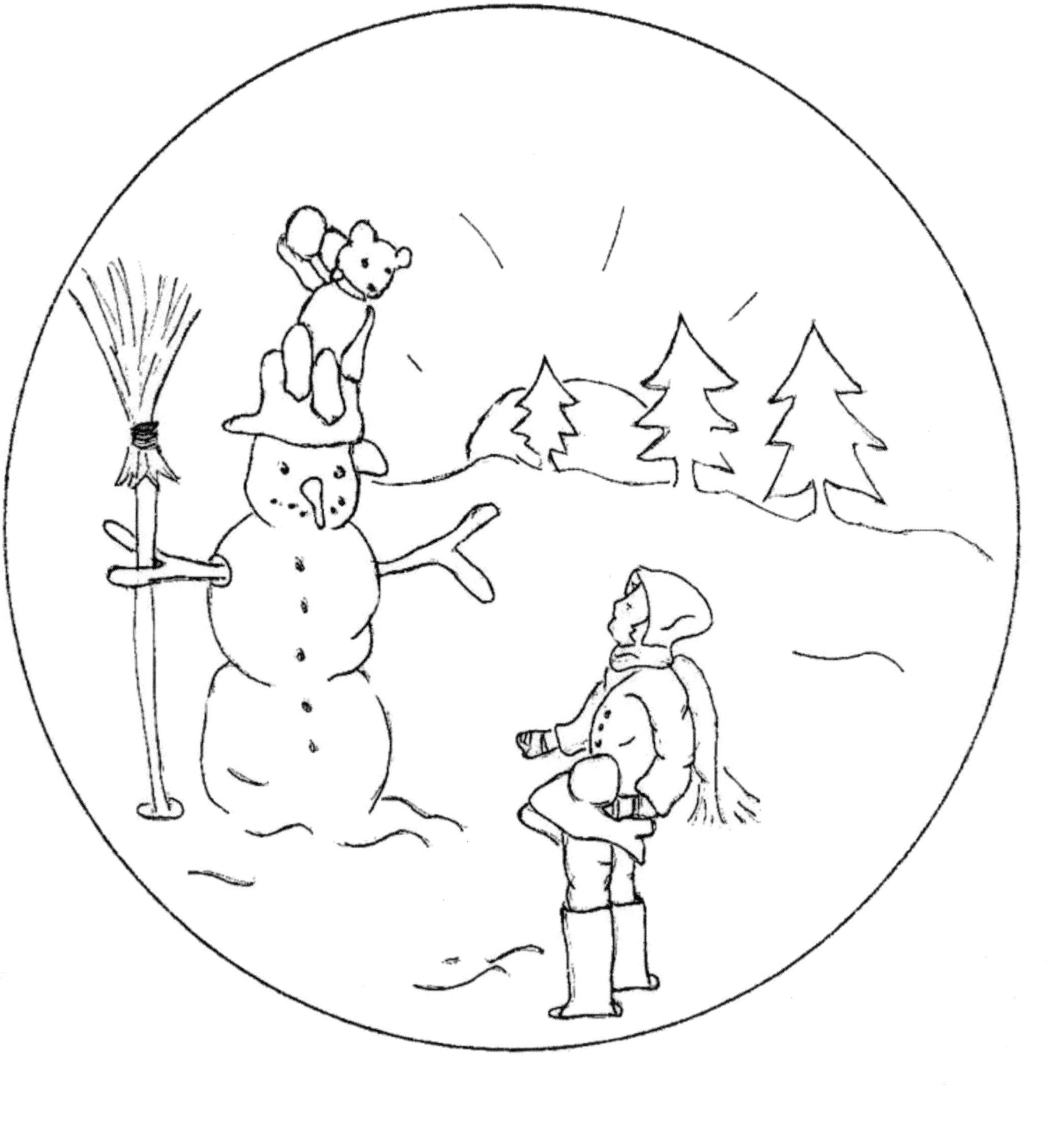

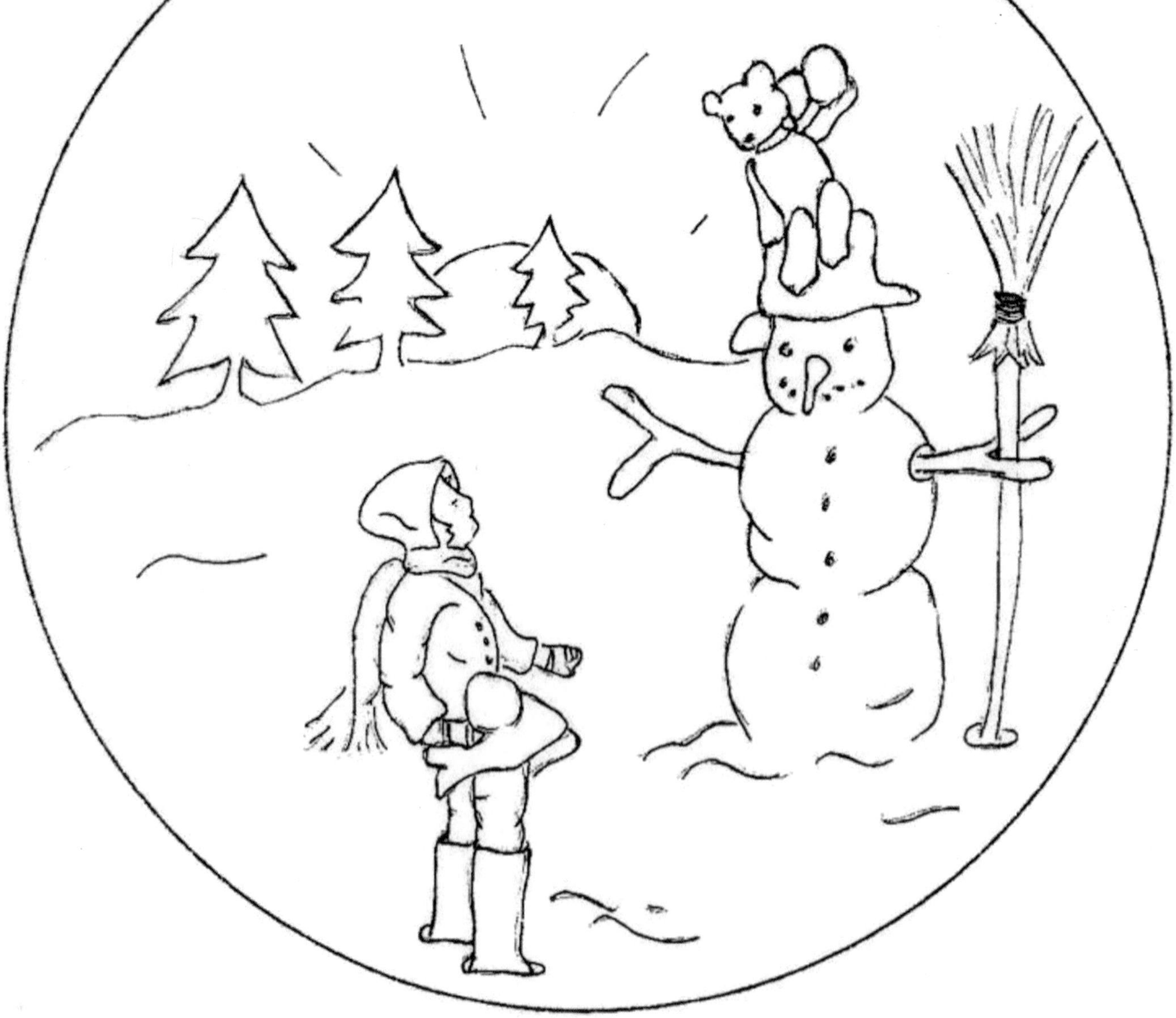

*"February brings the rain,
Fills the frozen lake again"*

FEBRUARY TRUE LOVE

February is well-known as an unsettled month, but here in England we often experience odd days of almost spring-like sunshine and crocuses and snowdrops appear, bringing signs that winter will soon be at an end. In the south we may also see early blossom in time for Valentine's Day on the 14th of the month.

Strangely, the celebration of Valentine's Day has no connection with St Valentine, except that the 14th is his Saint's Day. There is an old superstition that birds started mating on Valentine's Day - and here are two rather large and oddly-shaped birds perched high up on a tree branch. But look - the naughty pair have carved their initials into the bark - Bear loves Rosie - forever!

MATERIAL REQUIREMENTS

FOR THE EMBROIDERY

12" square cream linen or linen/cotton blend

DMC floss in colours ecru, 166, 315, 386, 504, 676, 704, 862, 3325, 3727, 3750, 3831, 3862, 4030, 4065, 4180, L833, blanc

STITCHES USED

Chain stitch, stem stitch, straight stitch, French knots, running stitch, back stitch.

Please see the Stitch Glossary at the back of this book if you are unfamiliar with working any of these stitches.

NOTES ON WORKING

For detailed instructions on working Bear's fur, please see the section "How to Embroider Fur" on page 17 of this book.

The design is worked in two strands of floss throughout unless otherwise stated.

Bear's ribbon is stitched in 4065 satin stitch. Change the direction of your satin stitch to delineate the knot and loops of his bow.

Rosie's features are worked in a single strand of dark brown.

Frame the design with running stitch using all 6 strands of 4030 You will probably need a larger needle to do this.

TIP OF THE MONTH

If you are unable to purchase the DMC floss used in this quilt, then you can substitute with a different brand, although the result won't be exactly the same.

You can find various conversion charts on line for many of the major brands, eg JP Coates, Anchor etc. Often the shades are close enough that nobody (except you!) will know that you've made the substitution.

Please don't use cheap floss though, it really isn't worth the economy and could end up spoiling your whole project if it shrinks or the colour runs in the wash - or even if it tangles and breaks as you work, making you too frustrated to continue with it!

Balloon 817 and ecru (highlight) concentric rings of chain stitch

String 3750 back stitch

Branch 3862 stem stitch

Leaves 704 and 166 detached chain stitch

Blossom 4180 French knots

Initials back stitch 1 strand 3831

Rosie:

Hair 3862 back stitch
Dress 3325 stem stitch
Collar 3727 back stitch
Skin 386 back stitch
Socks 504 back stitch
Shoes 315 back stitch

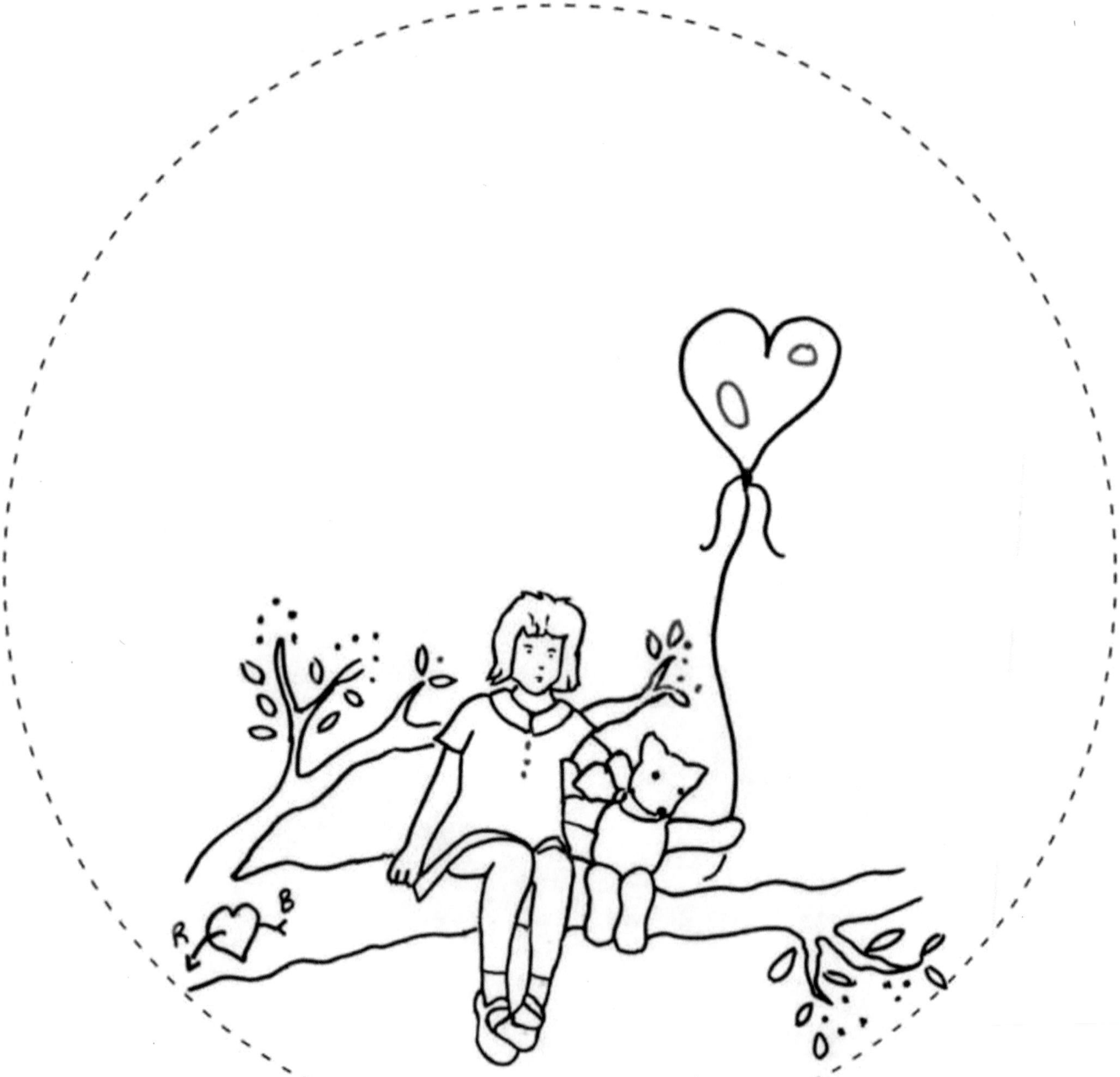
R
B

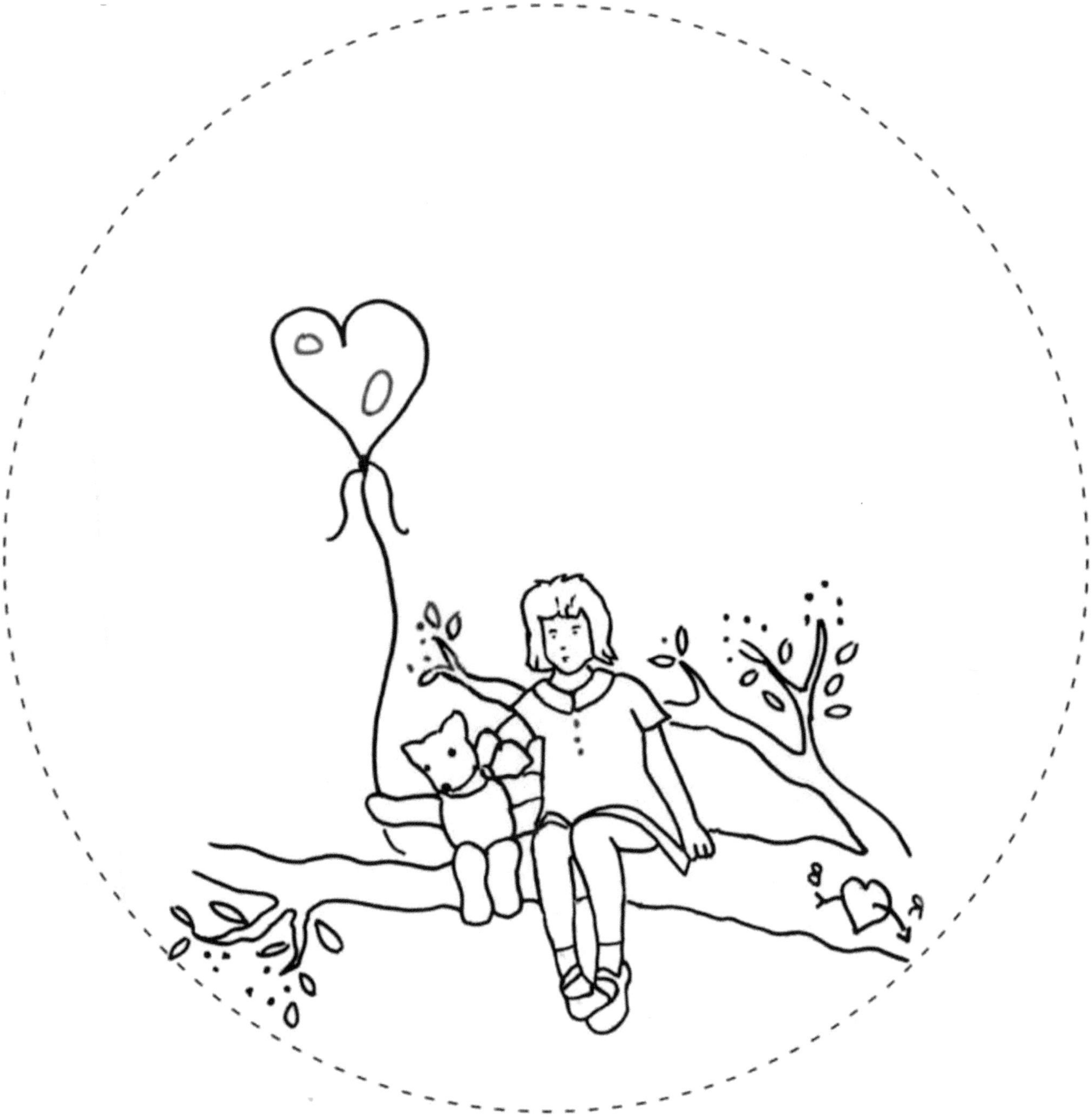

*"March brings breezes sharp and chill,
Shakes the dancing daffodil"*

MARCH SPRING LAMBKINS

In Saxon times - more than 1,000 years ago - March was called "Lenet-monat" which means "Length month." This recognises that in March at last the days are significantly longer and with the equinox falling around the 21st, the hours of daylight begin to exceed those of darkness. These days March is also the lambing season, and the fields around our village are filled with the sounds of mother ewes calling to their new baby lambkins.

Rosie is making friends with a pair of spring lamb twins, but Bear is not at all sure that they are harmless. He's staying well out of their reach and enjoying the fun from his perch up on the old ivy hedge.

MATERIAL REQUIREMENTS

FOR THE EMBROIDERY

12" square cream linen or linen/cotton blend

DMC floss in colours 310, 386, 504, 581, 676, 704, 838, 862, 3325, 3727, 3782, 4070, L833, blanc

STITCHES USED

Stem stitch, straight stitch, French knots, running stitch, back stitch.

Please see the Stitch Glossary at the back of this book if you are unfamiliar with working any of these stitches.

NOTES ON WORKING

For detailed instructions on working Bear's fur, please see the section "How to Embroider Fur" on page 17 of this book.

The design is worked in two strands of floss throughout unless otherwise stated.

Bear's ribbon is stitched in 4065 satin stitch. Change the direction of your satin stitch to delineate the knot and loops of his bow.

Rosie's features are worked in a single strand of dark brown.

Frame the design with running stitch using all 6 strands of 4070. You will probably need a larger needle to do this.

TIP OF THE MONTH

If using stranded floss to do your work, separate each strand from the whole and then put them back together to get more "fluff" from the threads and better coverage. This will also untwist the threads from one another so they will lie flat if you're working stitches such as satin or stem stitch.

Try to be sure to put them back together in the original orientation (ie which end was cut.) If threads are too fluffy to put through the eye of your needle, fold them over the needle and pinch between your fingers to fit through the eye. Only moisten the end of your thread as a last resort, and then use as little moisture as possible.

Rosie
Hair 3862 back stitch
Dress 3325 stem stitch
Collar 3727 back stitch
Shoes 315 back stitch
Skin 386 back stitch
Socks 504 back stitch
Flowers in hair small straight stitches in colours of your choice

Flower heads 3325, 4070 French knots

Leaves 704 & 581 straight stitch

Leaves 704 & 581 back stitch

Bear's ribbon 4065 satin stitch

Lambs' wool 3782 French knots

Hooves and faces 838 back stitch

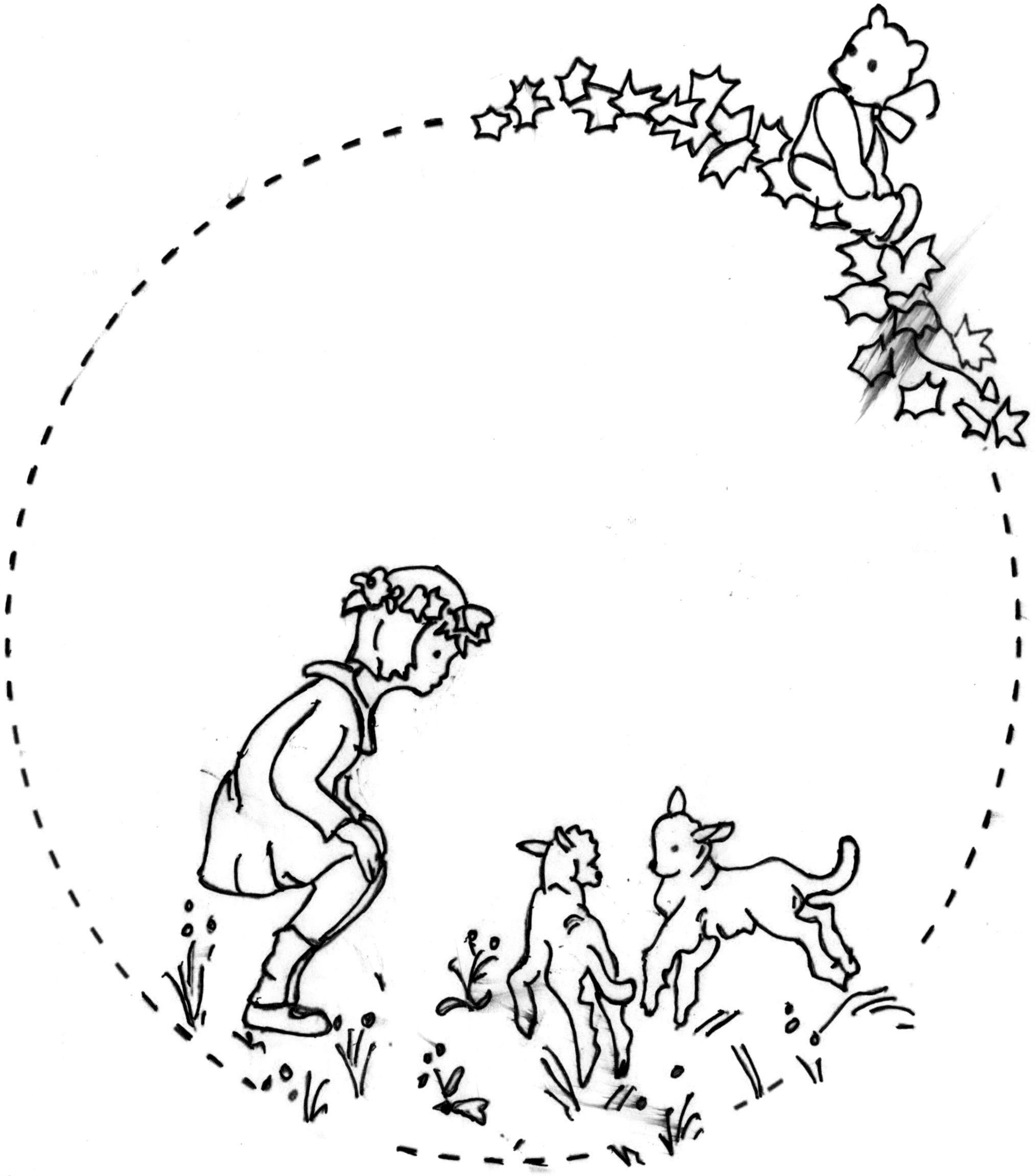

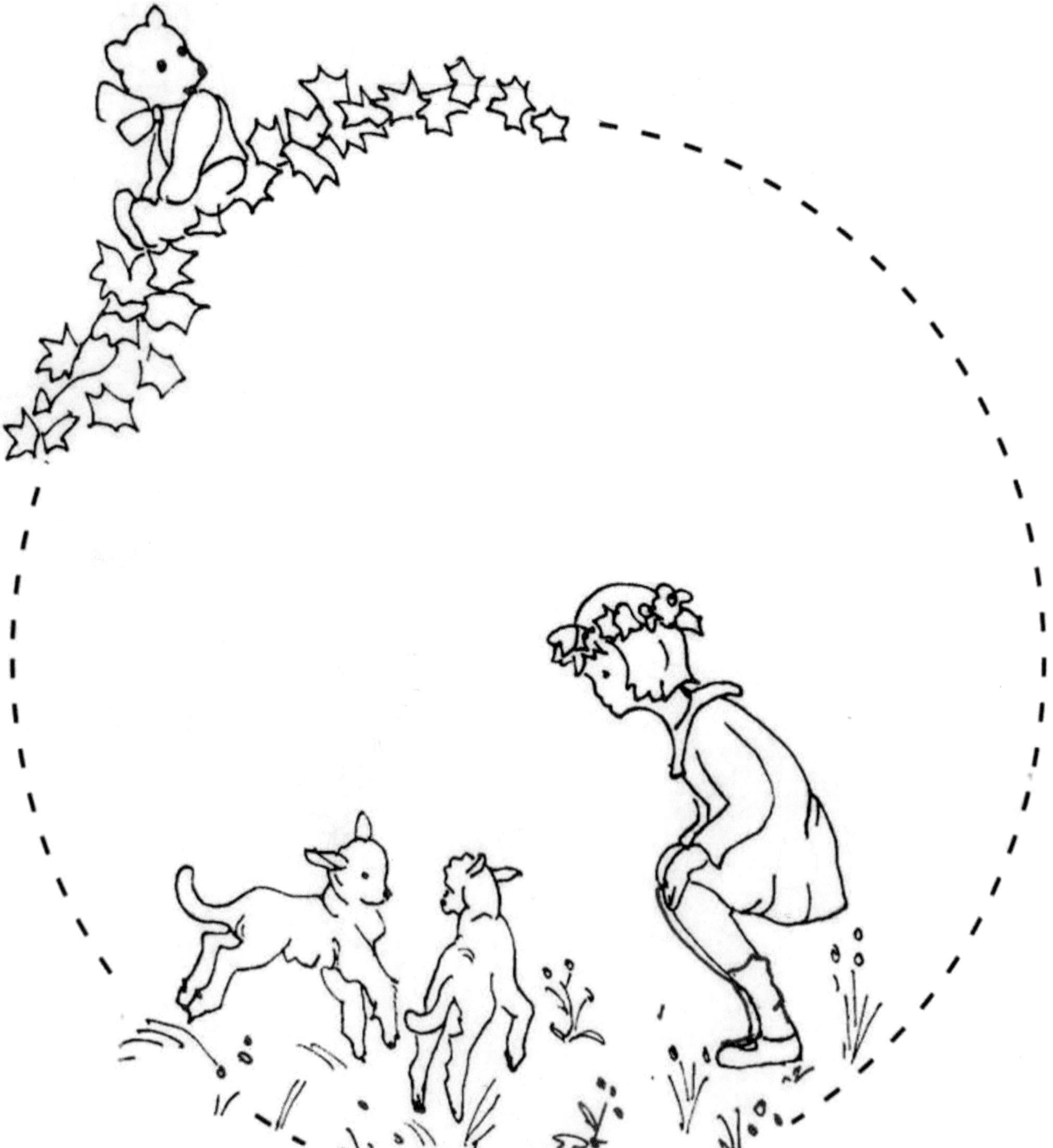

*"April brings the primrose sweet,
Scatters daisies at our feet"*

APRIL SPRING FLOWERS

April weather is a mixture of sun and showers - gardeners call it good growing weather because the sun begins to warm the ground whilst the soft showers water it. Trees are rapidly coming into leaf and many are in blossom. There are wild flowers in the hedgerows - cuckoo-pint, dog violets and buttercups are all blooming in the English hedgerows while the first baby birds are hatching.

Bear is proudly showing Rosie the beautiful spring flowers he has found, while up in the tree Mother Bird is watching as her babies call for her to bring them more nice fat juicy worms!

MATERIAL REQUIREMENTS

FOR THE EMBROIDERY

12" square cream linen or linen/cotton blend

DMC floss in colours 111, 257, 310, 315, 386, 504, 676, 704, 775, 839, 973, 3726, 3750, 3325, 3862, 4050, 4065, 4080, L833, blanc

STITCHES USED

Chain stitch, stem stitch, straight stitch, French knots, running stitch, back stitch, detached chain stitch (lazy daisy stitch).

Please see the Stitch Glossary at the back of this book if you are unfamiliar with working any of these stitches.

NOTES ON WORKING

For detailed instructions on working Bear's fur, please see the section "How to Embroider Fur" on page 17 of this book.

The design is worked in two strands of floss throughout unless otherwise stated.

Bear's ribbon is stitched in 4065 satin stitch. Change the direction of your satin stitch to delineate the knot and loops of his bow.

Rosie's features are worked in a single strand of dark brown.

Frame the design with running stitch using all 6 strands of 4080. You will probably need a larger needle to do this.

TIP OF THE MONTH

There are times when your stitching doesn't go right and you have to stop and unpick your work. This happens to all stitchers. It is not good. It is not fun. But sometimes it is necessary.

Don't be put off though – if you believe in what you're doing then it will all come right in the end. Just work through those times when nothing goes right, and you find yourself unpicking again and again, and you'll be rewarded with the thrill everything work out according to plan, the delight of seeing your creation grow and its various come together as a harmonious whole.

It's so satisfying to make something completely unique to you – in this age of mass production, a handmade, one-off, piece is very precious both to its maker and any lucky recipient.

Baby and mother birds 3862 back & straight stitch

Beaks & feet 973 back stitch

Nest 111, 839, 3862 small randomly-placed straight stitches

Trunk 839, 3862 stem stitch

Grass 704 straight stitch
Flowers 973 & 3726 straight stitches

Birds straight stitch 1 strand 3750

Leaves 257 & 704 detached chain stitch

Hills 4050 chain stitch

Rosie
Hair 3862 back stitch
Dress 3325 stem stitch
Cardigan 3726 stem stitch
Skin 386 back stitch
Shoes 315 satin stitch
Socks 504 back stitch

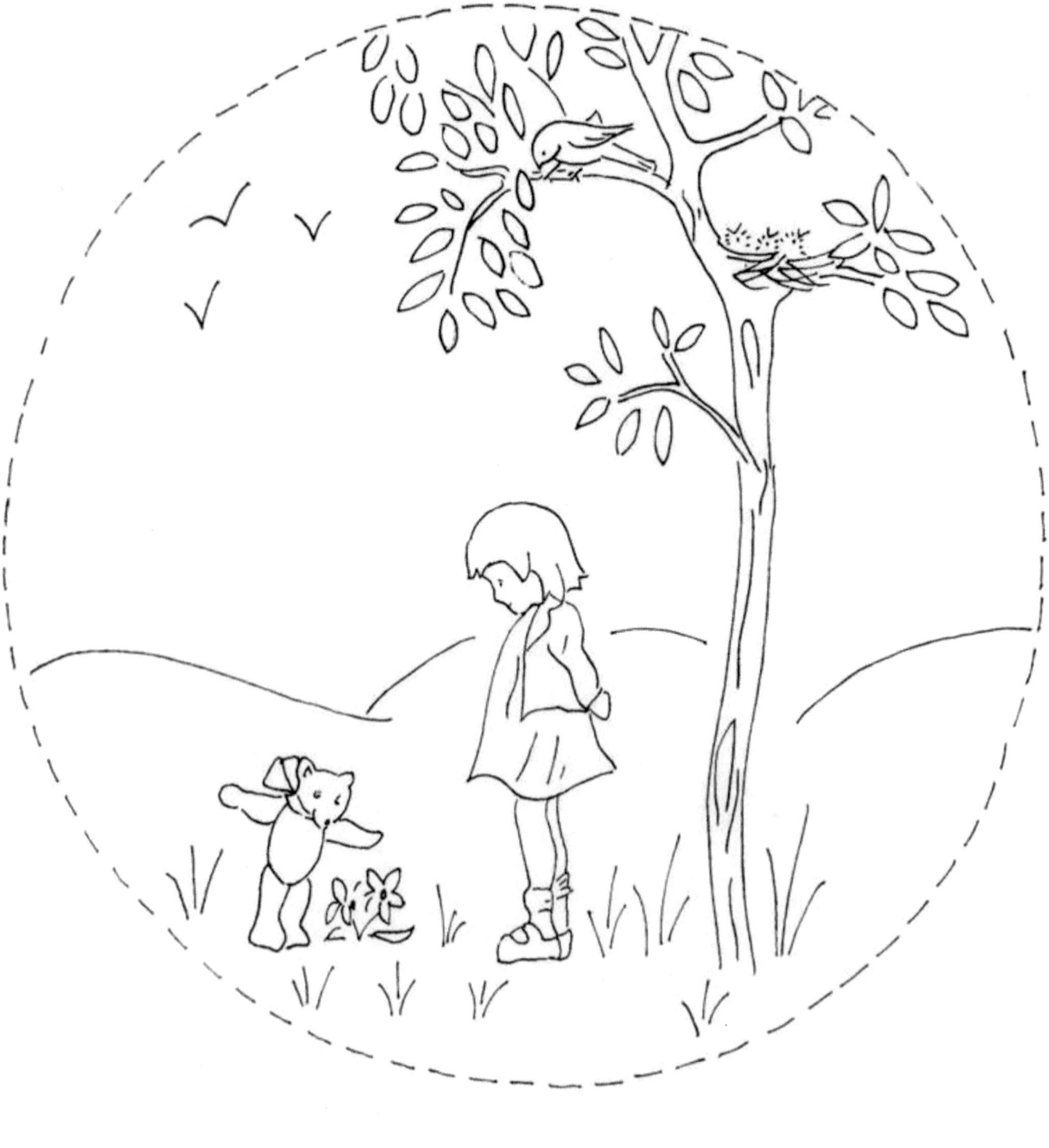

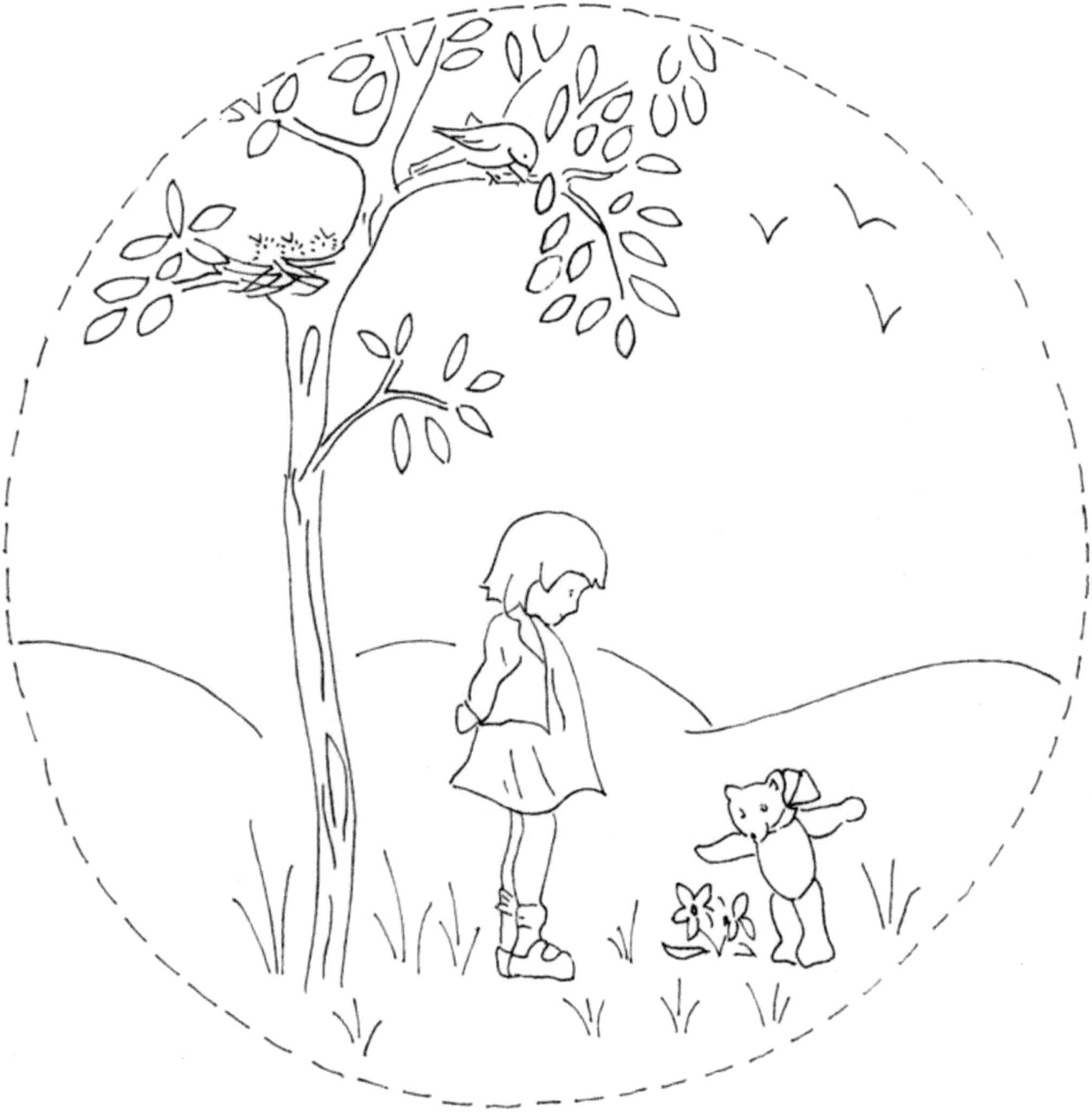

*"May brings flocks of pretty lambs,
Sporting round their fleecy dams"*

MAY BLOSSOM TIME

These days lambing has finished by May and the sheep are all out in the fields again. May is one of the most beautiful months of the year here in England. It can feel as warm as summer, and there are flowers in abundance, though there can often be bitterly cold winds, sometimes blowing the blossom off the trees before the fruit has had time to set.

In this block Rosie and Bear are enjoying a warm spring day, and it's not the wind blowing the blossom from the trees, but Bear, who has picked a huge bunch for Rosie and now is having fun dropping more blooms down onto her head!

MATERIAL REQUIREMENTS

FOR THE EMBROIDERY

12" square cream linen or linen/cotton blend

DMC floss in colours 386, 518, 676, 704, 775, 907, 3706, 3726, 3862, 4060, 4065, 4100, 4070 L833 blanc

STITCHES USED

Stem stitch, straight stitch, satin stitch, running stitch, back stitch.

Please see the Stitch Glossary at the back of this book if you are unfamiliar with working any of these stitches.

NOTES ON WORKING

For detailed instructions on working Bear's fur, please see the section "How to Embroider Fur" on page 17 of this book.

The design is worked in two strands of floss throughout unless otherwise stated.

Bear's ribbon is stitched in 4065 satin stitch. Change the direction of your satin stitch to delineate the knot and loops of his bow.

Rosie's features are worked in a single strand of dark brown.

Frame the design with running stitch using all 6 strands of 4070. You will probably need a larger needle to do this.

TIP OF THE MONTH

Don't forget - if you're stitching with a hoop, then to stop your fabric slipping, bind the inner hoop with fabric strips, cotton tape or bias binding and secure the end with a few stitches. If you're working with fabric that is easily marked or damaged then you might choose to bind the outer hoop too.

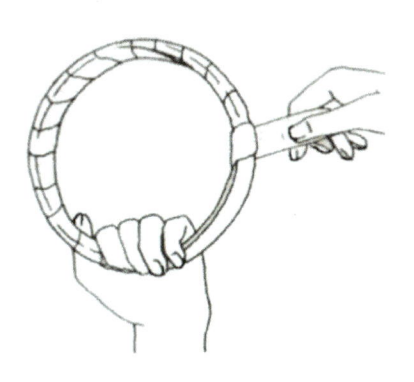

Bouquet and garland

The flowers are tiny straight stitches, or you could use a small French knot if you prefer, with radiating straight stitches for the petals.

The leaves are worked in satin stitch.

When working the blossoms work the flower centres first. They are worked in 518 and 3706 (mix randomly). Don't worry if there are small gaps between the flowers, fill in with the leaves and work small straight stitches if any gaps are left.

Leaves
704 and 907

Flowers
Petals 4100 & 4060 (mix randomly)
Centres 518 and 3706 (mix randomly)

Rosie
Hair 3862 back stitch
Dress 3726 stem stitch
Skin 386 back stitch
Collar 775 stem stitch

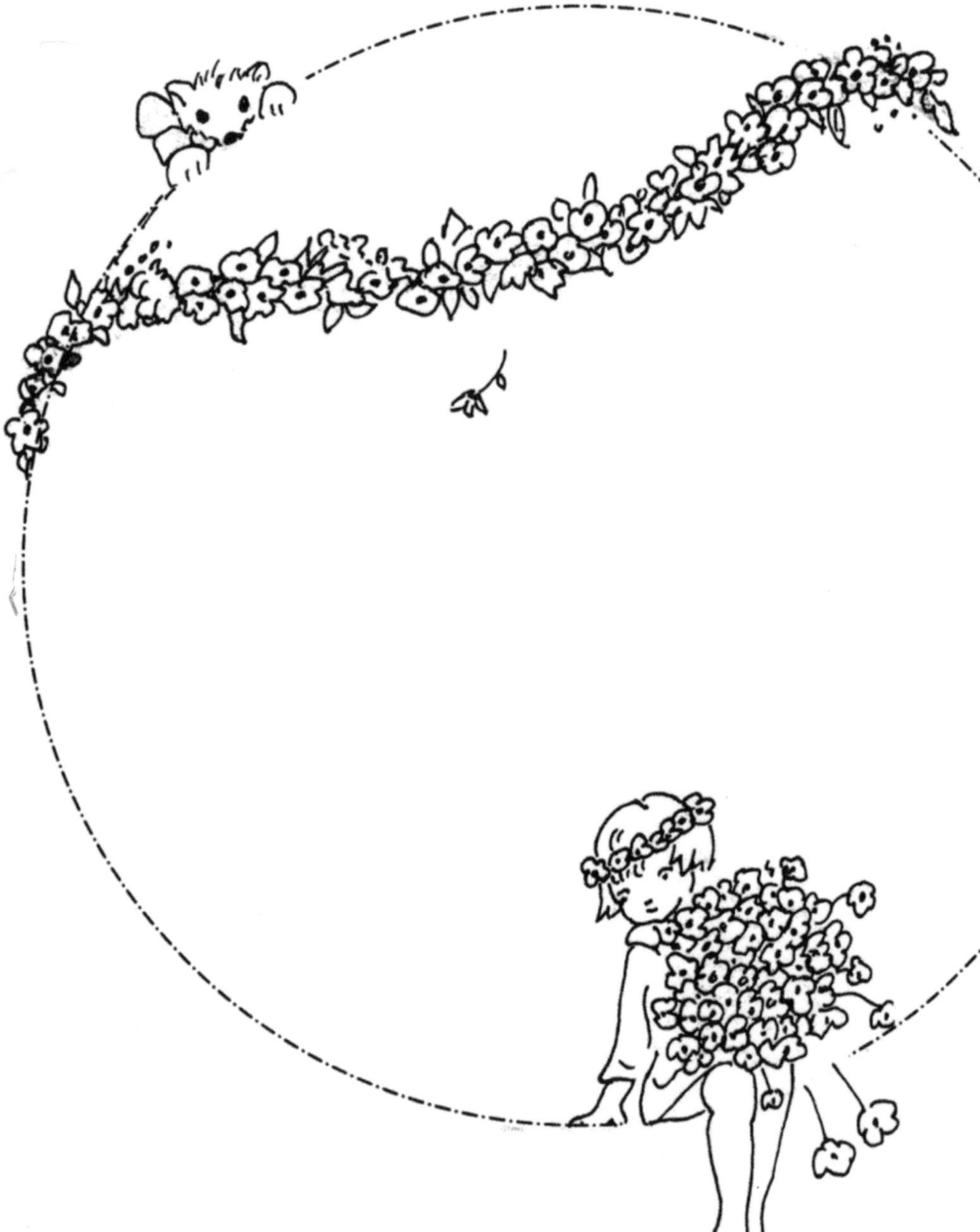

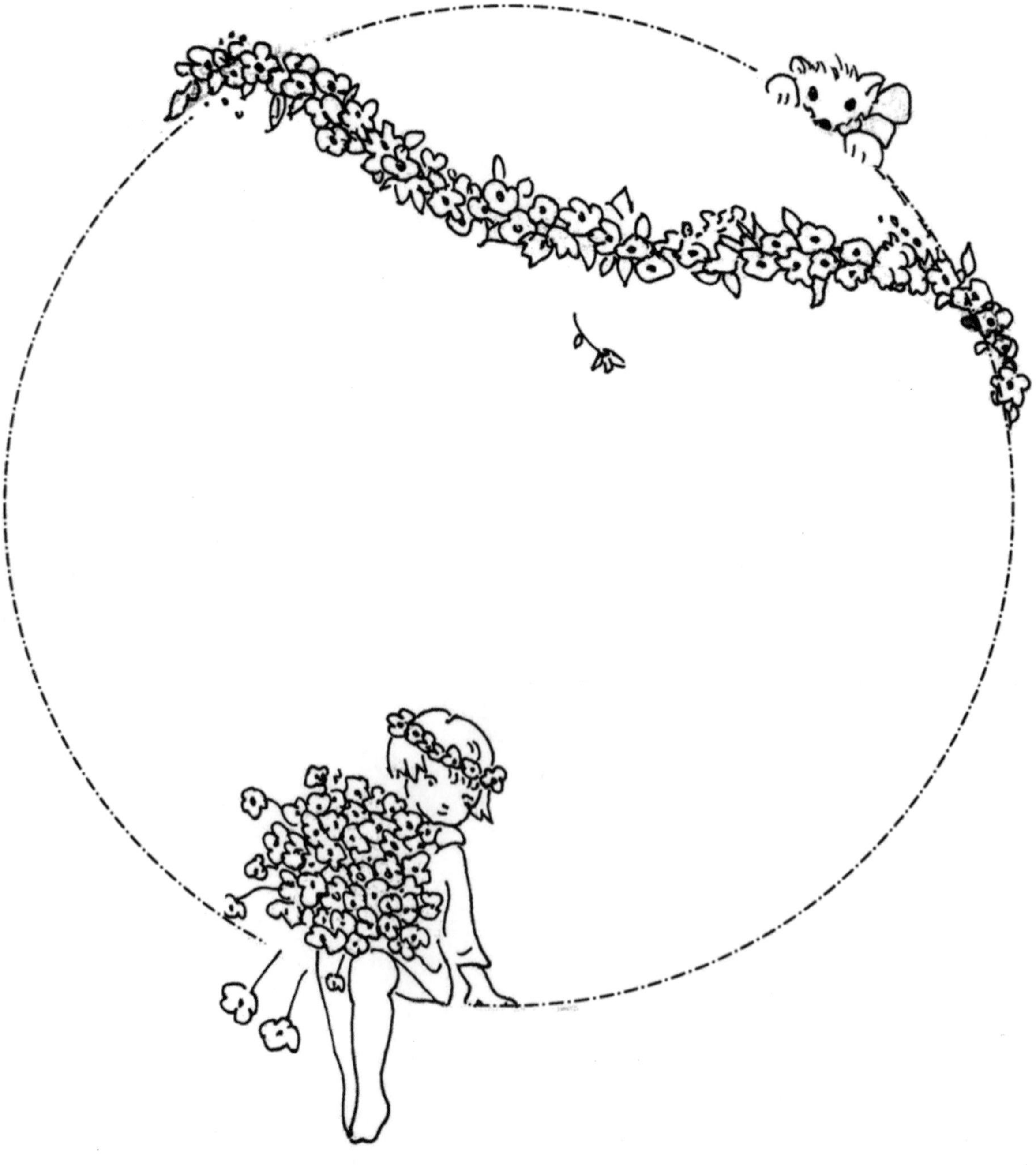

*"June brings tulips, lilies, roses,
Fills the children's hands with posies."*

JUNE SUMMER BEDTIME

By June all the trees are in full leaf, but the foliage is still young and fresh and looks intensely green. Everywhere the bees are busy, and walking along the country lanes you can hear them in the foxgloves that grow in tall purple spikes in the hedgerows.

This month the days are at their longest and the nights are short - which inspired this quilt block with lines from the poem by R L Stevenson. Rosie really doesn't want to be tucked up in bed while it's still light outside and naughty Bear is calling her to "Come outside and play!"

MATERIAL REQUIREMENTS

FOR THE EMBROIDERY

12" square cream linen or linen/cotton blend

DMC floss in colours 315, 347, 386, 434, 676, 740, 761, 906, 935, 3325, 3031, 3802, 3862, 3841, 4065, 4190, L833, blanc

STITCHES USED

Stem stitch, straight stitch, French knots, running stitch, back stitch, satin stitch.

Please see the Stitch Glossary at the back of this book if you are unfamiliar with working any of these stitches.

NOTES ON WORKING

For detailed instructions on working Bear's fur, please see the section "How to Embroider Fur" on page 17 of this book.

The design is worked in two strands of floss throughout unless otherwise stated.

Bear's ribbon is stitched in 4065 satin stitch. Change the direction of your satin stitch to delineate the knot and loops of his bow.

The quilt blocks are worked in the floss colours given, plus very small amounts of yellow and dark blue - such very tiny amounts I haven't included them in the list above. If you do need to purchase them, I used 445 and 158, but substituting them with colours you do have is absolutely fine.

Frame the design with running stitch using all 6 strands of 4065. You will probably need a larger needle to do this.

TIP OF THE MONTH

When completing any project keep a note of the name of the fabric and the number and type of thread used in the construction of the piece for future reference.

If buttons are used in the design, then a spare button tucked inside is also a nice touch.

Window frame 3325 back stitch

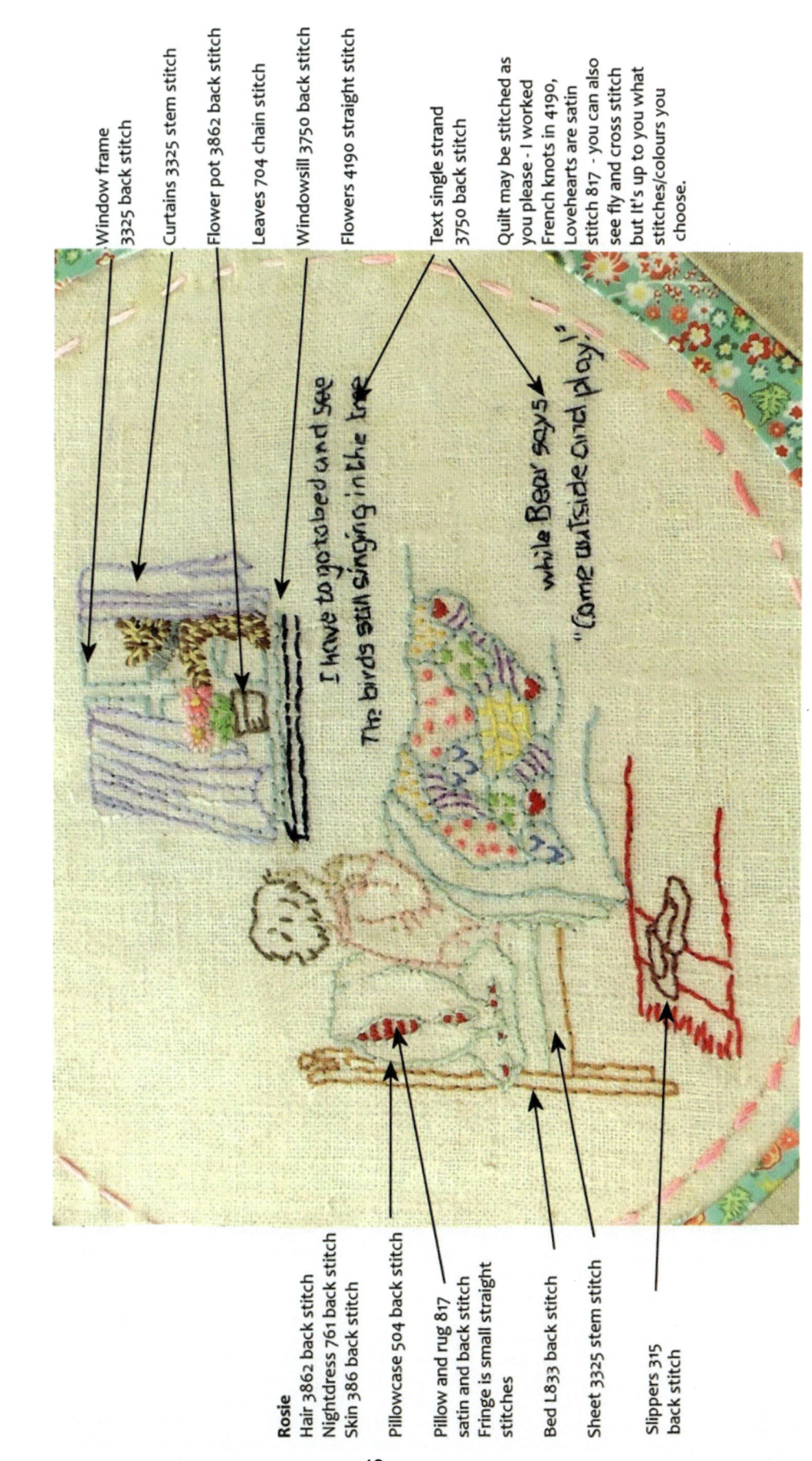

Curtains 3325 stem stitch

Flower pot 3862 back stitch

Leaves 704 chain stitch

Windowsill 3750 back stitch

Flowers 4190 straight stitch

Text single strand 3750 back stitch

Quilt may be stitched as you please - I worked French knots in 4190, Lovehearts are satin stitch 817 - you can also see fly and cross stitch but it's up to you what stitches/colours you choose.

Rosie
Hair 3862 back stitch
Nightdress 761 back stitch
Skin 386 back stitch

Pillowcase 504 back stitch

Pillow and rug 817 satin and back stitch
Fringe is small straight stitches

Bed L833 back stitch

Sheet 3325 stem stitch

Slippers 315 back stitch

I have to go to bed and see
The birds still singing in the tree,

while Bear says,
"Come outside and play!

I have to go to bed and see
The birds still singing in the tree,

while Bear says,
"Come outside and play!"

*"Hot July brings cooling showers,
Apricots and gillyflowers."*

JULY FAIRGROUND CAROUSEL

There is colour everywhere this month. Over the ley dragonflies dart, their brilliant irridescent colours passing in a flash. Wild mint and scabious bring more colour along the bank whilst butterflies flutter over the flowers. The Scarlet Pimpernel, a tiny flower that grows in dusty places, is fully out when the weather is sunny. If rain threatens - and July is known for thunderstorms - its petals close. It is known as the "poor man's weather glass".

July is also the month that the travelling fairground visits the town near us. Round and round twirl the carousel horses, Rosie clinging tightly to the pole whilst that naughty Bear shows off by balancing on just one paw!

MATERIAL REQUIREMENTS

FOR THE EMBROIDERY

12" square cream linen or linen/cotton blend

DMC floss in colours 310, 315, 386, 518, 676, 758, 907, 938, 3021, 3041, 3325, 3705, 3726, 3768, 3862, 4065, 4075, L833, blanc

STITCHES USED

Stem stitch, straight stitch, buttonhole stitch, running stitch, back stitch, cross stitch.

Please see the Stitch Glossary at the back of this book if you are unfamiliar with working any of these stitches.

NOTES ON WORKING

For detailed instructions on working Bear's fur, please see the section "How to Embroider Fur" on page 17 of this book.

The design is worked in two strands of floss throughout unless otherwise stated.

Bear's ribbon is stitched in 4065 satin stitch. Change the direction of your satin stitch to delineate the knot and loops of his bow.

Rosie's features are worked in a single strand of dark brown.

Frame the design with running stitch using all 6 strands of 4065. You will probably need a larger needle to do this.

TIP OF THE MONTH

Keep the back of your embroidery work neat by not allowing thread to "travel" more than ¼ or 3/8 inch. Instead turn your work over, and "weave" the thread over to the new starting point to begin again from there.

This also keeps thread from showing through to the front of an embroidery (important when working lightweight, pale fabrics such as the calendar blocks in this quilt).

The flags each have a tiny cross stitch in the centre in the same colour as one of the adjacent flags. I have given the horse gold highlights on his hooves (optional)

Flag colours 907, 3705, 4075, 518 back stitch
String 315 back stitch

The horse's harness is worked in the same colours as the flags in back stitch, apart from the saddlecloth which is worked in buttonhole stitch and 2-coloured chain stitch.

Mane, tail and hooves 3041 stem and back stitch

Pole straight stitch 4075

Horse body 3768 stem stitch

Rosie
Hair 3862 back stitch
Top 3726 stem stitch
Skirt 3325 stem stitch
Skin 386 back stitch

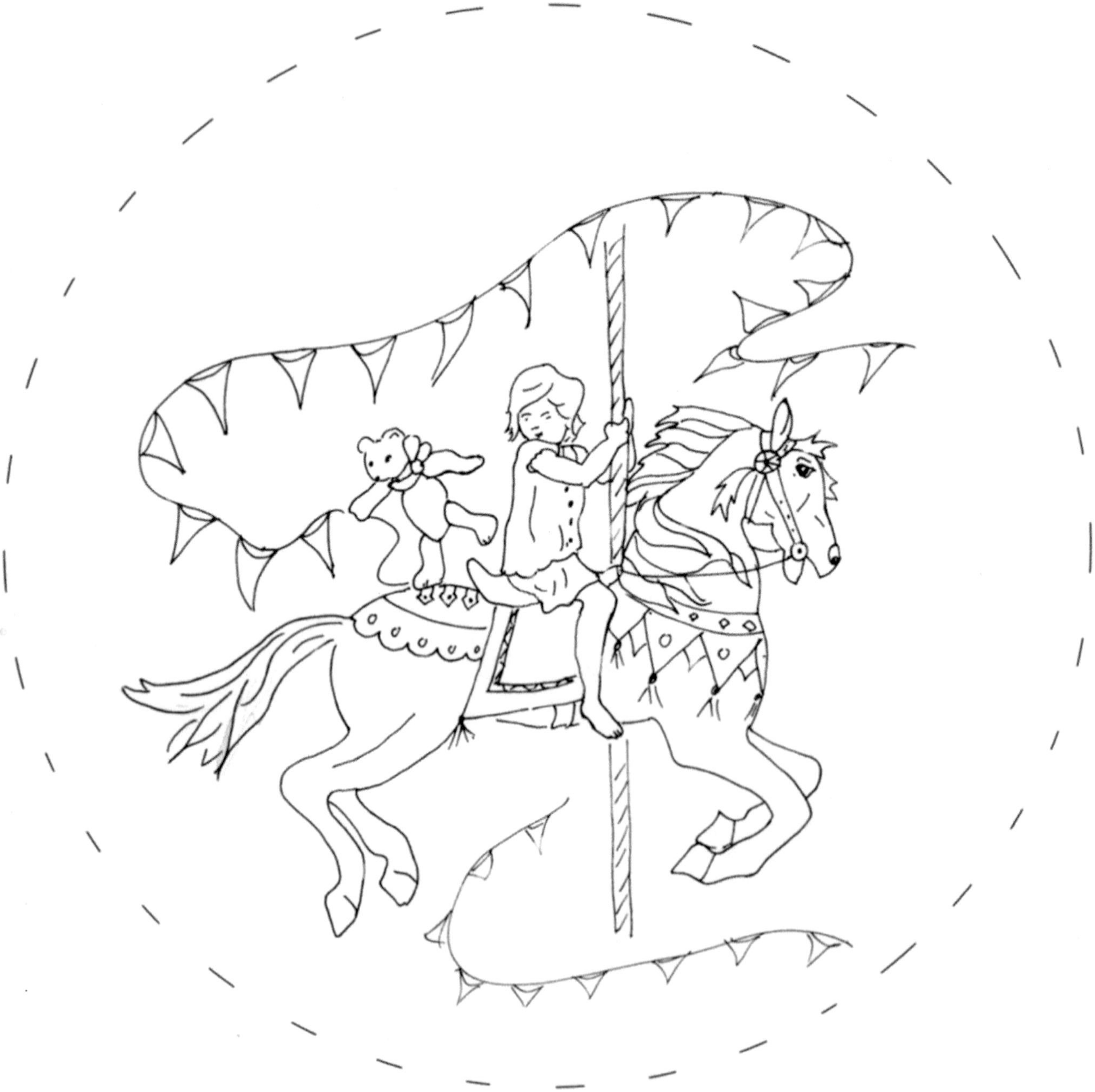

*"August brings the sheaves of corn,
Then the harvest home is borne."*

AUGUST AT THE BEACH

August is the time to visit the seaside and spend long happy hours shrimping, exploring rock pools and munching on sandy sandwiches! Slimy seaweed underfoot brings lots of excited squeals from children, but in fact it serves a very useful purpose by covering the rocks with a damp blanket, protecting the creatures that live there from the heat of the summer sun.

Rosie and Bear are having fun paddling and building sandcastles, though I think Bear is showing off again - and is very likely to return home with rather damp and sandy fur at the end of the day!

MATERIAL REQUIREMENTS

FOR THE EMBROIDERY

12" square cream linen or linen/cotton blend

DMC floss in colours 310, 315, 386, 676, 680, 862, 3325, 3750, 3851, 3862, 4030, 4065, 4070, L833, blanc

STITCHES USED

Straight stitch, back stitch, stem stitch, buttonhole stitch, running stitch.

Please see the Stitch Glossary at the back of this book if you are unfamiliar with working any of these stitches.

NOTES ON WORKING

For detailed instructions on working Bear's fur, please see the section "How to Embroider Fur" on page 17 of this book.

The design is worked in two strands of floss throughout unless otherwise stated.

Bear's ribbon is stitched in 4065 satin stitch. Change the direction of your satin stitch to delineate the knot and loops of his bow.

Rosie's features are worked in a single strand of dark brown.

Frame the design with running stitch using all 6 strands of 4070. You will probably need a larger needle to do this.

TIP OF THE MONTH

Stitching can be a fun, social activity, as well as something you do by yourself at quiet times. Why not consider joining a group of stitchers with the same interest as you. You can learn from each other and give tips and pointers while you are working on your project.

Ask at your local embroidery store or quilt shop if they know a group you can join. Use the internet – there are thousands of possibilities on there. Look for links to other stitchers' websites and blogs, patterns, tutorials, classes etc. Join online forums and meet online with other embroiderers.

Boat and sandcastle flags
3831 satin or straight stitch

Sail 4065 back stitch

Boat 3831 back stitch

Sandcastles 680 back stitch

Net 4065 buttonhole stitch

Handle 3750 satin stitch

Sea 4030 stem stitch

Rosie
Hair 3862 back stitch
Dress 315 stem stitch
Collar 3325 back stitch
Skin 386 back stitch

*"Warm September brings the fruit,
Sportsmen then begin to shoot."*

SEPTEMBER IN THE APPLE TREE

September is a month of change - we still experience some hot sunny days but with early morning mists and chilly evenings that tell us autumn is on the way. Blackberries are everywhere this month and mushrooms are easily found. The best time to gather them is in the very early morning as they spring up on cool misty nights.

Apples are also abundant in September - as Bear has discovered. The naughty pair are sitting in the old apple tree at the end of the Orchard (where they're not supposed to be) and Bear has found a beautiful shiny red apple that he's sure Rosie will enjoy.

MATERIAL REQUIREMENTS

FOR THE EMBROIDERY

12" square cream linen or linen/cotton blend

DMC floss in colours 257, 277, 310, 321, 386, 676, 704, 754, 775, 815, 838, 839, 3862, 4065, 4128, L833, blanc

STITCHES USED

Stem stitch, straight stitch, satin stitch, French knots, running stitch, back stitch, detached chain stitch (lazy daisy).

Please see the Stitch Glossary at the back of this book if you are unfamiliar with working any of these stitches.

NOTES ON WORKING

For detailed instructions on working Bear's fur, please see the section "How to Embroider Fur" on page 17 of this book.

The design is worked in two strands of floss throughout unless otherwise stated.

Bear's ribbon is stitched in 4065 satin stitch. Change the direction of your satin stitch to delineate the knot and loops of his bow.

Frame the design with running stitch using all 6 strands of 4075. You will probably need a larger needle to do this.

TIP OF THE MONTH

The ascent of the stitcher

Most of the history of sewing is of work stitched by hand – from the simplest stitches to wonderful decorative work – until the first functioning sewing machine appeared – patented by Barthelemy Thimonnier in France in 1830.

But the sewing machine as we know (and love) it today didn't appear until the 1850's when Singer built the first truly successful sewing machine.

Centre of apples
tiny French knot in 704

Apples 815 and 321
satin stitch

Rosie
Hair 3862 back stitch
Dress 775 stem stitch
Skin 386 back stitch
Collar 4065 back stitch

Tree 839, 277 stem stitch

Leaves 257 and 704
detached chain stitch

Hills 4080 stem stitch

Field boundary 4128
chain stitch

Cabbages 704
French knots

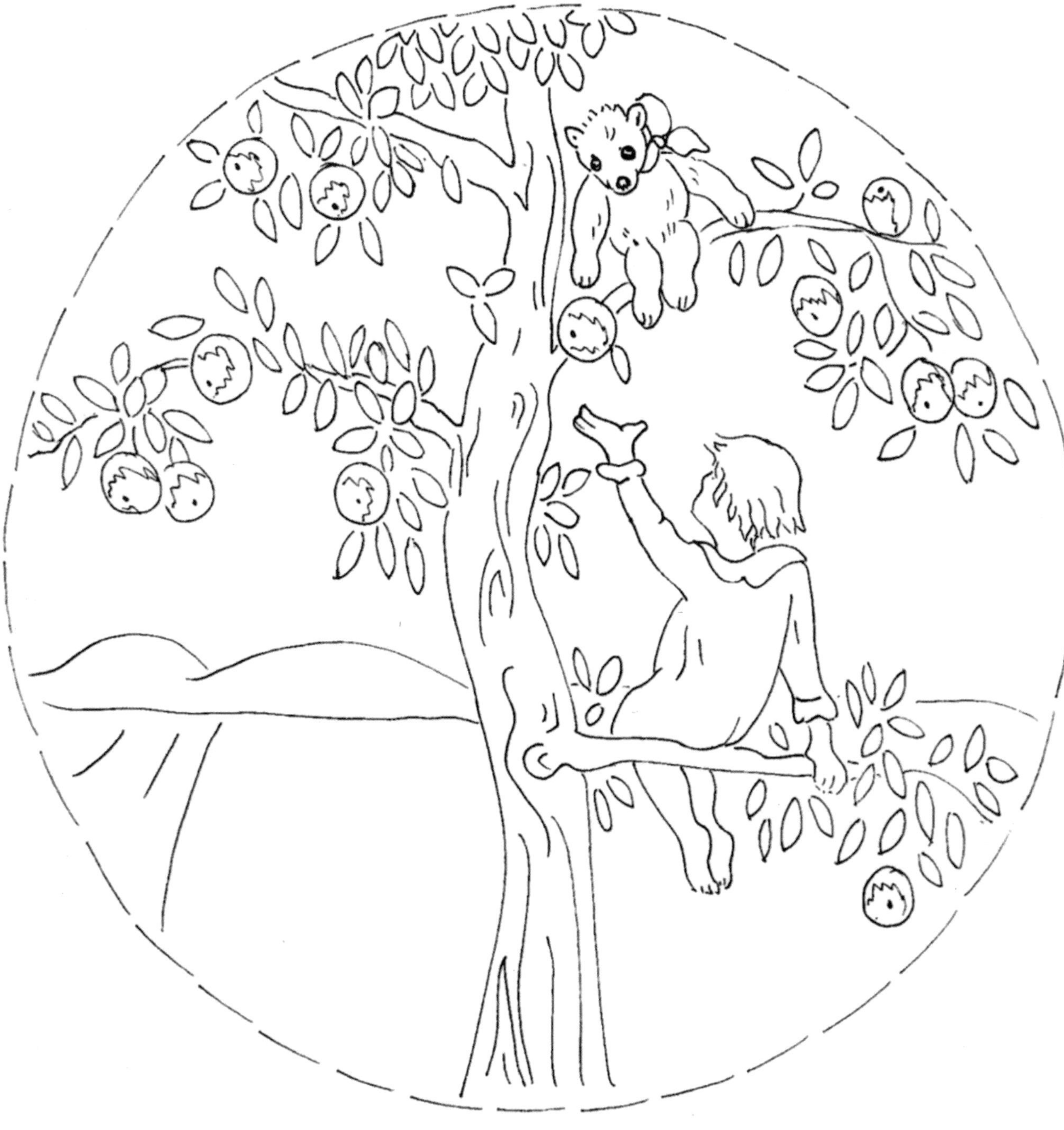

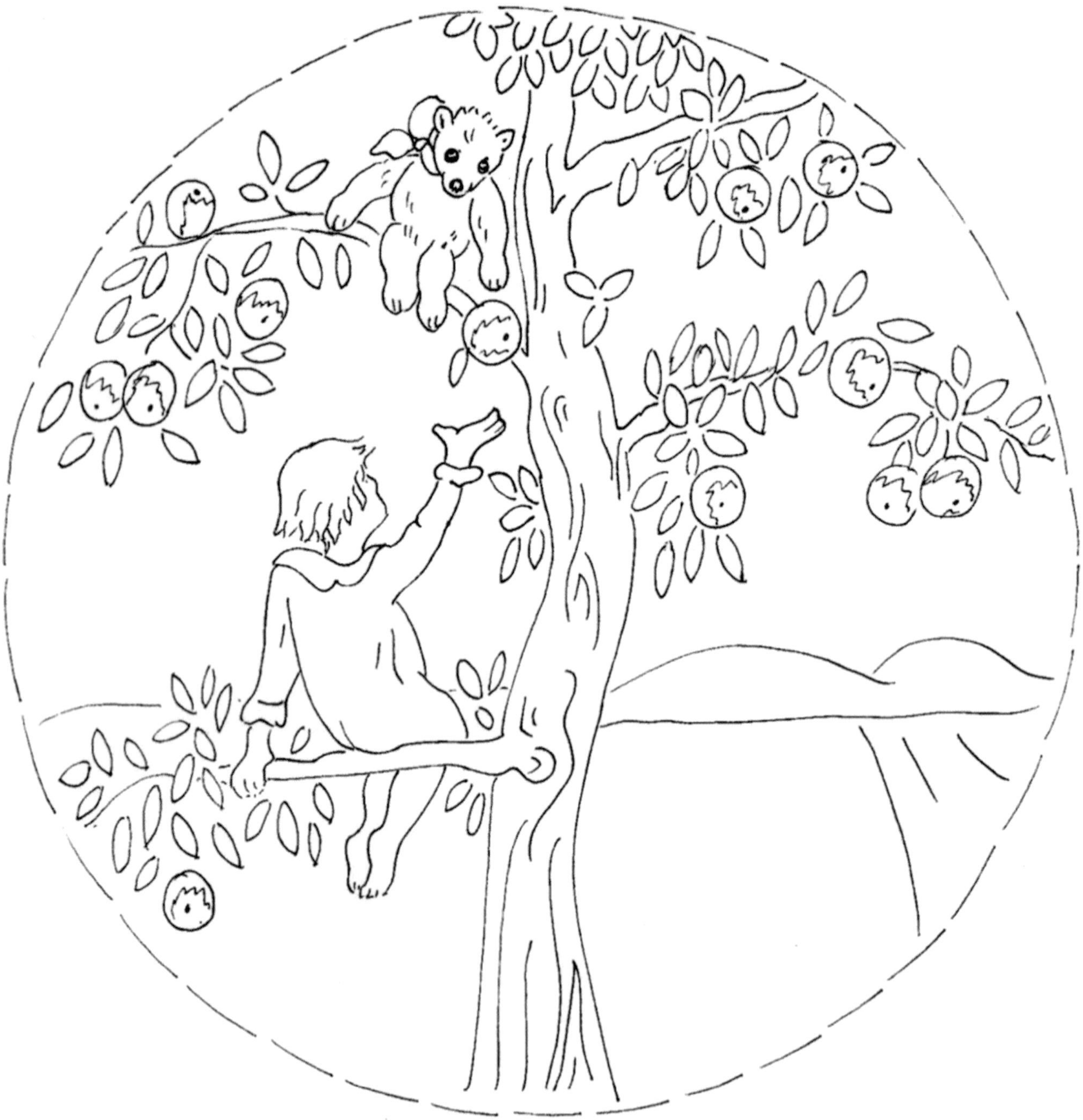

*"Brown October brings the pheasant,
Then to gather nuts is pleasant."*

OCTOBER HALLOWEEN PARTY

In the woods the leaves are falling quickly now and the summer-visiting birds have left for warmer places. October 31st is All Hallows Eve, also called Halloween, the day before All Saints Day. Celebrating this date goes back to pagan times and nobody knows when this tradition started. It was believed that on this night all sorts of supernatural creatures were around.

We still hold Halloween parties and enjoy playing many of the old games, such as apple bobbing. Here Rosie and Bear are enjoying their very own Halloween party with masks, hats and streamers adding to the fun.

MATERIAL REQUIREMENTS

FOR THE EMBROIDERY

12" square cream linen or linen/cotton blend

DMC floss in colours 310, 386, 504, 667, 729, 742, 862, 904, 906, 977, 3325, 3727, 3276, 3862, 4065, 4126, L833, blanc

STITCHES USED

Straight stitch, back stitch, stem stitch, buttonhole stitch, running stitch, French knots, long and short Stitch.

Please see the Stitch Glossary at the back of this book if you are unfamiliar with working any of these stitches.

NOTES ON WORKING

For detailed instructions on working Bear's fur, please see the section "How to Embroider Fur" on page 17 of this book.

The design is worked in two strands of floss throughout unless otherwise stated.

Bear's ribbon is stitched in 4065 satin stitch. Change the direction of your satin stitch to delineate the knot and loops of his bow.

Rosie's features are worked in a single strand of dark brown.

Frame the design with running stitch using all 6 strands of 4126. You will probably need a larger needle to do this.

TIP OF THE MONTH

When stitching you don't have to limit yourself to fabric – if your chosen vice is embroidery you'll find you can stitch on almost anything.

I've seen some lovely creations stitched onto old maps, pages from vintage books and even patterns formed by threading twine through holes in stones.

If you can push fibre through it then you can embroider it!

Streamers stem stitch 742 (yellow), 906 (green), 3726 (violet), 720 (orange)

Rosie

Hair 3862 back stitch
Dress & shoes 3726 back and stem stitch
Collar and dots on dress 3727 back/satin stitch
Skin 386 back stitch
Socks 504 back stitch
Mask and hat 310 back stitch
Patches on hat 906, 720 and 742
Buttons & closure on dress tiny stitches 1 strand 3726

Bear's hat is worked in long & short stitch - start with the dots in 977 and then work the green around them

Rosie's hat is outlined in 310 back stitch then multi coloured pompoms & patches are added.

Pumpkin back stitch 720 features straight stitch 977
chain 904 chain stitch
fittings 904 back/straight stitch

Long streamer 4126 satin stitch

Bear's feather 742 straight stitch

Hat 906 and 977 long & short stitch

Bear's trumpet 906 & 720 back stitch

Confetti - randomly sprinkle 906, 742 and 720 satin stitch

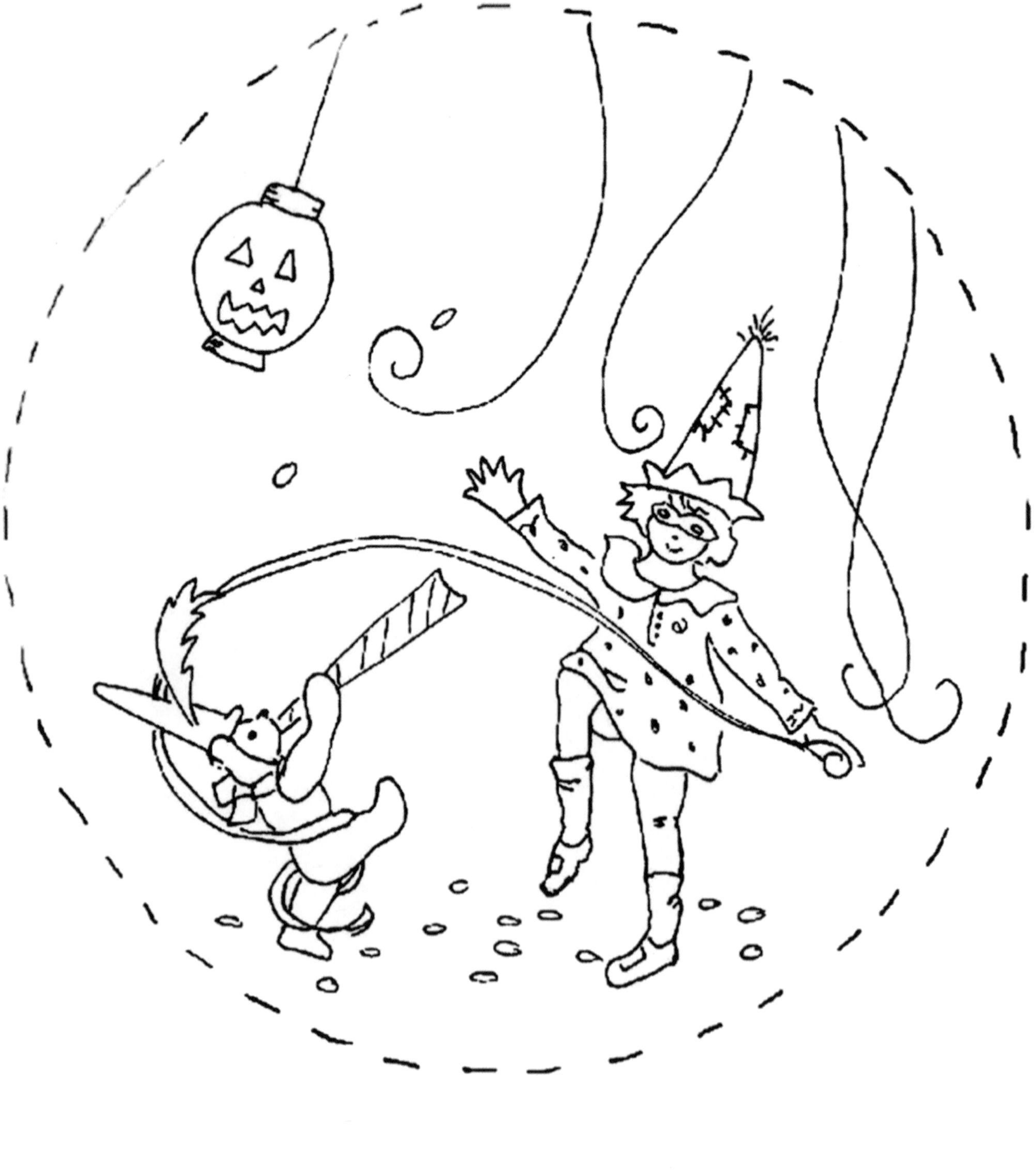

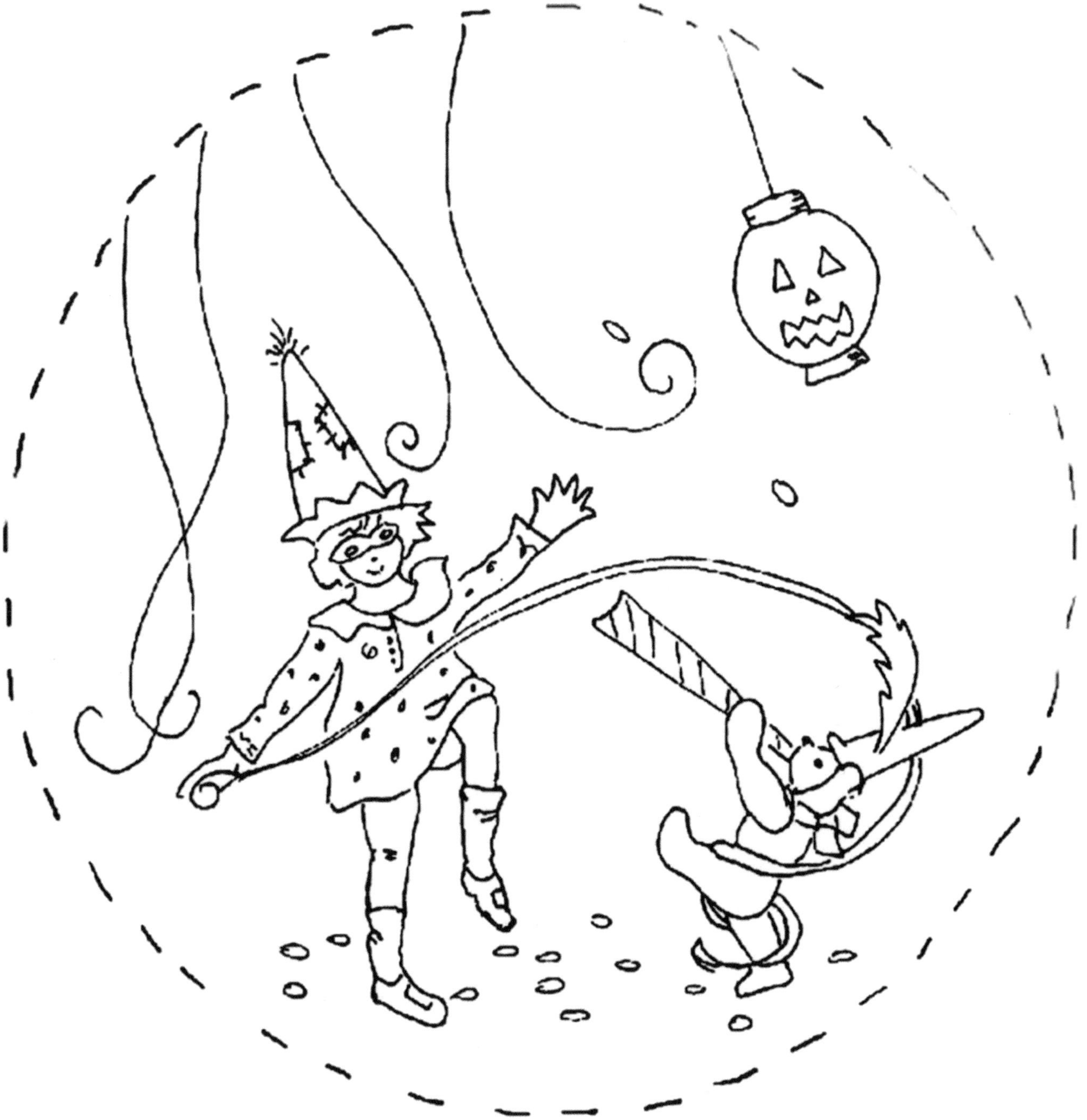

*"Dull November brings the blast,
Hark the leaves are whirling fast."*

NOVEMBER RAINY DAY

November is a damp and frosty month. The days are much shorter now and the colour seems to have been drained from the world. It is the month for ploughing and as the farmer in his tractor turns the soil to reveal long chocolate-brown furrows, the air is filled with the cries of seagulls who follow him, looking for worms and grubs that have been turned up.

Rosie and Bear don't seem to be too worried about the rain. Bear has found a very large umbrella that he's using to shelter Rosie from the downpour. I am sure that before too long she'll slip on her wellies and head off to splash around in the puddles!

MATERIAL REQUIREMENTS

FOR THE EMBROIDERY

12" square cream linen or linen/cotton blend

DMC floss in colours 257, 310, 386, 676, 775, 3726, 3325, 3862, 4065 L833, blanc. Thrifted crochet mat for clouds (optional).

STITCHES USED

Stem stitch, straight stitch, running stitch, back stitch, detached chain stitch.

Please see the Stitch Glossary at the back of this book if you are unfamiliar with working any of these stitches.

NOTES ON WORKING

For detailed instructions on working Bear's fur, please see the section "How to Embroider Fur" on page 17 of this book.

The design is worked in two strands of floss throughout unless otherwise stated.

Rosie's features are worked in a single strand of dark brown.

Bear's ribbon is stitched in 4065 satin stitch. Change the direction of your satin stitch to delineate the knot and loops of his bow.

Frame the design with running stitch using all 6 strands of 4065. You will probably need a larger needle to do this.

The clouds are made with thrifted crochet mats painted with fabric paints (follow the manufacturer's instructions). Then cut your mat in two, position on embroidery and trim cut edges to circle shape. Machine zig-zag edges in place and then catch down the scalloped edges of the mat with tiny stitches. If you don't want to use a mat, then stitch the clouds in chain stitch and 4065.

TIP OF THE MONTH

Ensure you have good lighting for the evenings or late afternoons in autumn & winter. I have made the mistake of mixing up black and dark blue far too many times for it to be funny!

A daylight bulb is best, easily obtained from good craft or needlework retailers.

Rosie
Hair 3862 back stitch
Skin 386 back stitch
Dress 3726 stem stitch
Collar 3325 back stitch

Umbrella 257 stem stitch
handle 3862 - 2 rows
of stem stitch

Rain drops 775
detached chain stitch

*"Cold December brings the sleet,
Blazing fire and Christmas treat"*

DECEMBER CHRISTMAS GIFT

Our quilt should really have begun with December, as it was one very special, long-ago Christmas that Rosie found Bear waiting for her under the tree on Christmas morning.

There are still berries to be gathered in the hedgerows, and of course most seasonal of all are the holly and mistletoe. Early in the mornings, if there has been a hoar frost overnight, everywhere will be covered in white and spiders' webs will sparkle in the early morning sun.

At the end of the short days when the low lying sun sets early, cold mist will often rise from the fields and settle in the dips and hollows, and over water.

MATERIAL REQUIREMENTS

FOR THE EMBROIDERY

12" square cream linen or linen/cotton blend

DMC floss in colours 257, 310, 315, 386, 504, 704, 973, 3727, 3862, 4065, 4080 L833, blanc

STITCHES USED

Straight stitch, back stitch, stem stitch, detached chain stitch, running stitch.

Please see the Stitch Glossary at the back of this book if you are unfamiliar with working any of these stitches.

NOTES ON WORKING

For detailed instructions on working Bear's fur, see the section "How to Embroider Fur" on page 17 of this book.

The design is worked in two strands of floss throughout unless otherwise stated.

Bear's ribbon is stitched in 4065 satin stitch. Change the direction of your satin stitch to delineate the knot and loops of his bow.

Rosie's features are worked in a single strand of dark brown.

Frame the design with running stitch using all 6 strands of 4080. You will probably need a larger needle to do this.

TIP OF THE MONTH

To keep thread, floss and yarn from tangling and knotting when sewing, every so often hold the tail of the medium with the needle dangling and let it unwind.

Another trick to keep thread, floss and yarn from tangling and knotting when sewing is to thread it through a bit of beeswax before starting, or thread it through thick unscented and non-tinted lip balm.

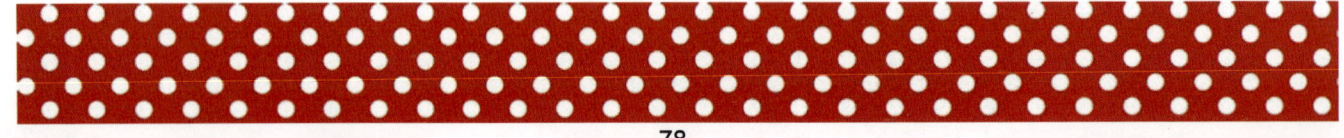

Rosie
Hair 3862 back stitch
Dress 3325 stem stitch
Petticoat 3727 back stitch
Skin 386 back stitch
Socks 504 back stitch
Shoes 315 satin stitch

Star 973 satin stitch

Tree stem stitch
257 dark green and
704 light green

Candle flames
973 satin stitch
halo around flame
973 straight stitch

Candles 315 straight stitch

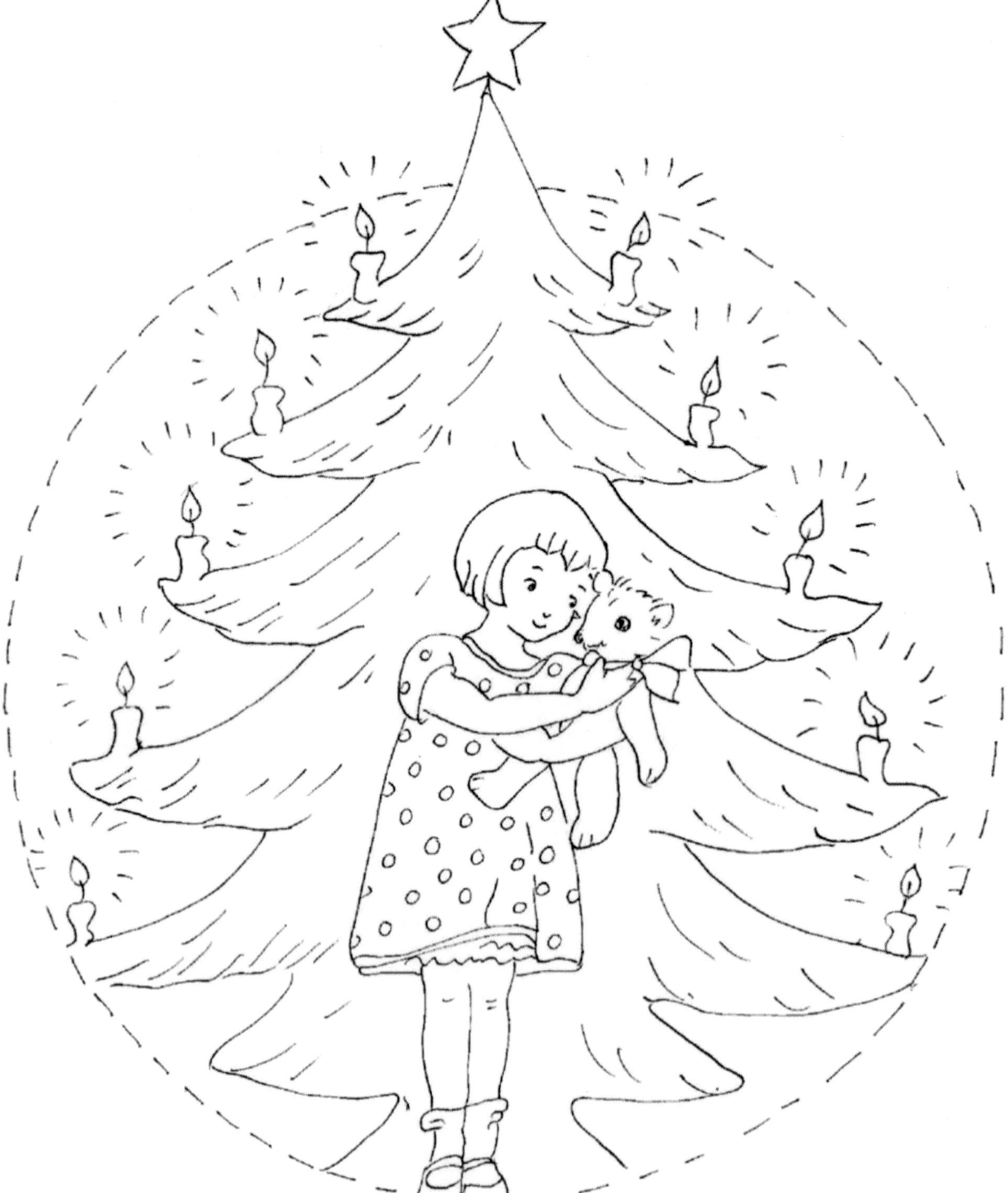

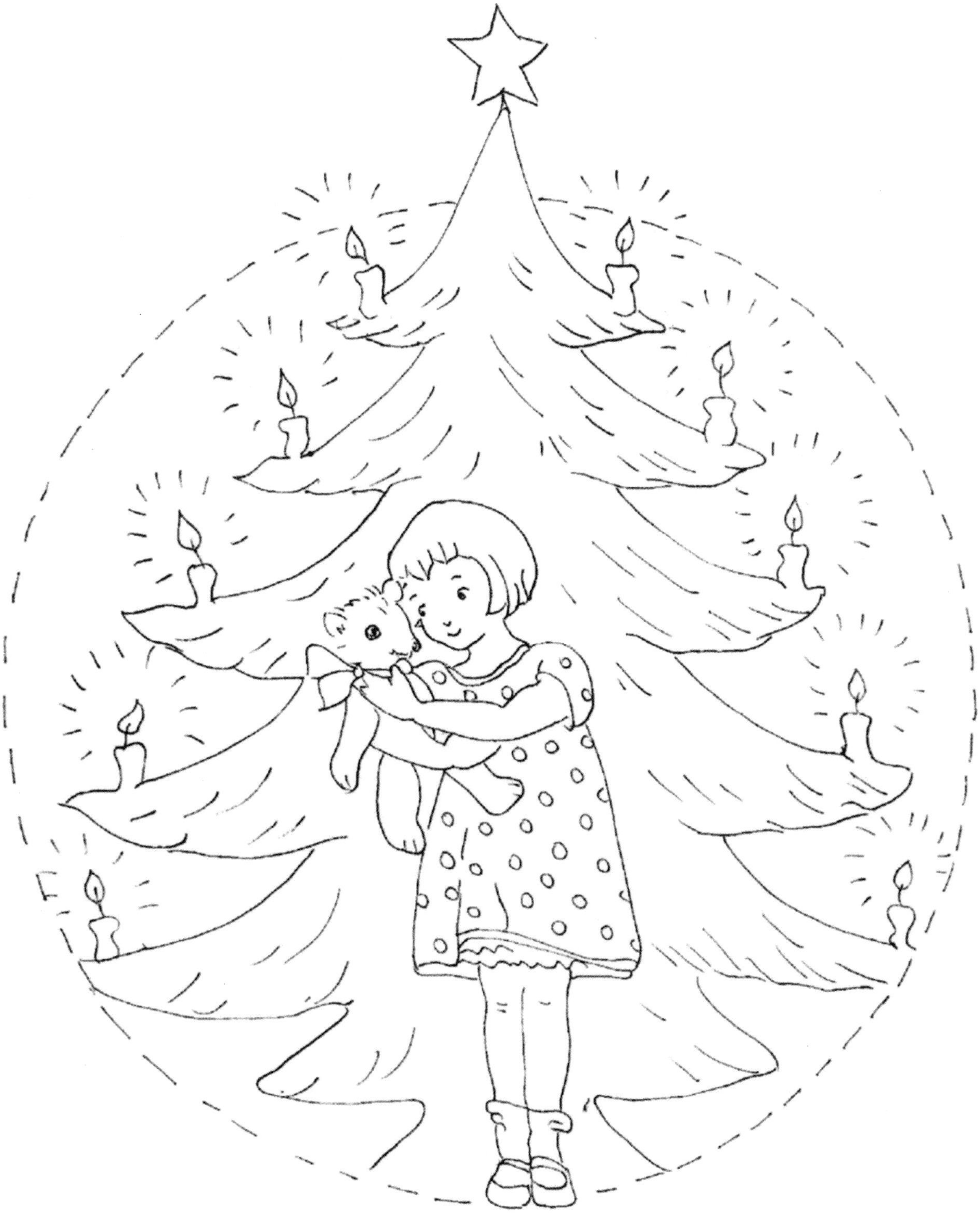

TESTING YOUR SEAM ALLOWANCE

It's vitally important that you maintain an accurate ¼" seam allowance when you're piecing your quilt top or otherwise your pieces simply won't fit together. And if you try to make them fit then you quilt will develop ripples and distortions that will make it impossible to finish properly.

It is well worth taking the time to test your seam allowance before you begin your quilt top, especially as you have invested so much time in stitching your calendar blocks.

Most sewing machines do have various needle positions which you can use to make any necessary adjustments, and some have ¼" and other markings on the needle plate too.

- Accurately cut 3 rectangles, each measuring 1 ½" x 2 ½" from scrap fabric

- Sew two rectangles together down the longer side and press your seam to one side.

- Now stitch the third rectangle across the top of the other two, aligning the long edge with the two short top edges (see diagram at the bottom of the page).

If the third rectangle doesn't fit across the top of the other two exactly then you'll need to adjust your seam allowance.

If the top rectangle is too long, then your seam allowance is too wide, and if it's too short then your seam allowance is too narrow.

You can adjust your seam allowance by resetting your needle to the right or left - or simply by taking care to follow the guide you normally find on your machine.

Take especial care at the ends of seams - I find my seams have a tendency to run off to the left, so distorting my shapes and so I'm now very careful not to let this happen. Accuracy is everything!!

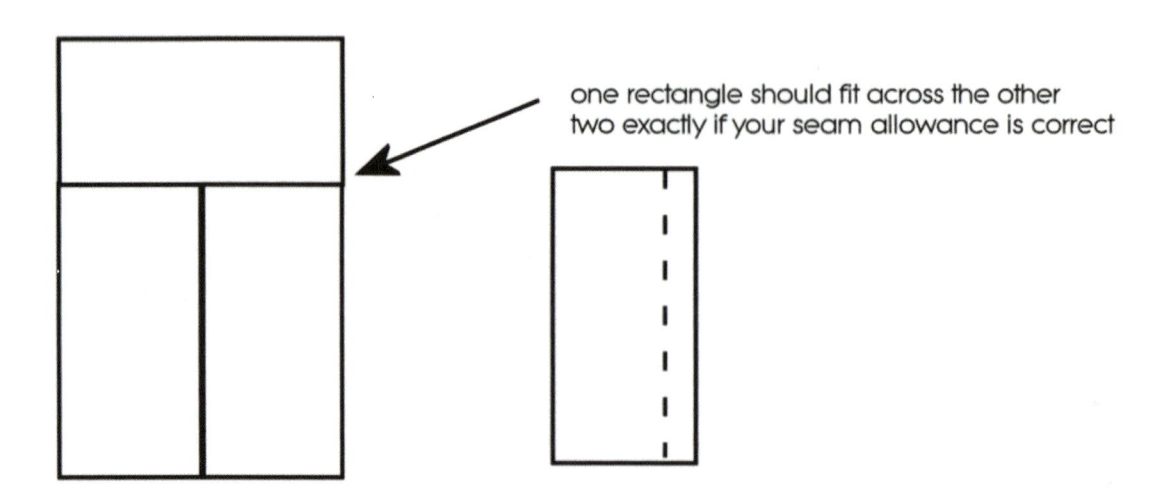

one rectangle should fit across the other two exactly if your seam allowance is correct

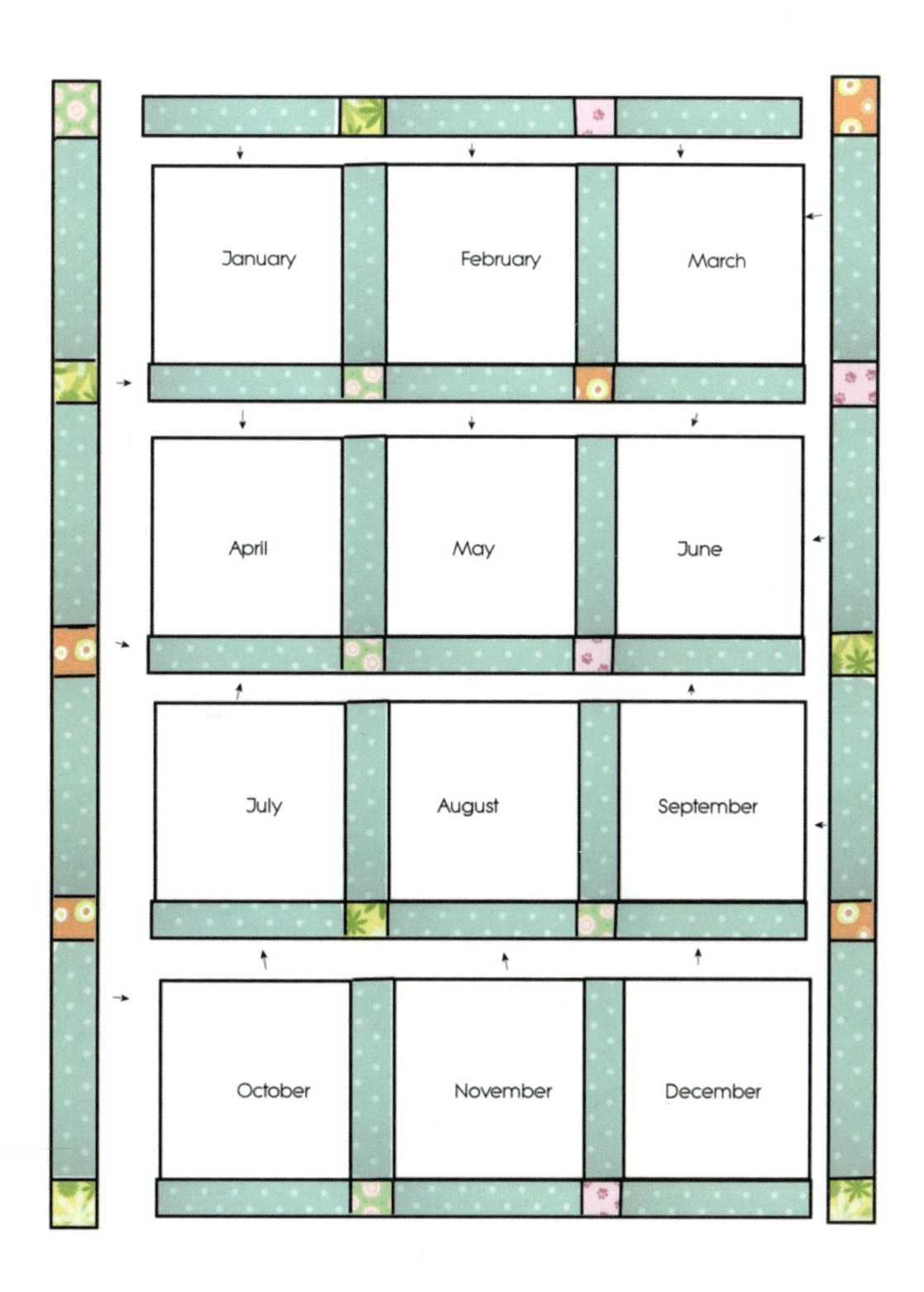

Diagram for piecing top (see page 84)

PIECING THE QUILT TOP

The importance of accuracy in cutting and piecing your quilt top cannot be overstated. If you cut wonky edges or sew an uneven seam allowance your quilt top will not lie flat. It will develop ripples in the borders or puckers in the fabric, or your pieces simply won't fit together properly. Please do take the time to read the previous section "Testing your Seam Allowance" before beginning this stage in your quilt construction.

I have given all measurements in inches. This is because an inch is still the standard unit used in quilting and giving alternative (not exactly the same) metric measurements simply doesn't work.

All seam allowances are ¼" unless otherwise stated.

You will see from the pictures of the finished quilt, that unusually the on-point squares have no points.

This is quite deliberate. I have called them "enfolded squares." I wanted to show in my quilt that Rosie, no matter where she was, or what she was doing, was surrounded by - enfolded by - her mother's love. By enfolding the blocks within the sashing I have also removed the sharp points - and I'm sure you'll agree with me that there is no room at all for sharp points in any loving parent-child relationship!

PREPARING YOUR EMBROIDERY BLOCKS

Before you start cutting your pieces you will need to prepare your embroidery blocks.

If necessary wash your work. Press all the blocks lightly on the reverse and ensure all ends are properly secured.

Then fold your block in 4 to find the centre point. Using a template trim your fabric to a 9" diameter circle centred upon the embroidery. This circle should fall about ½" outside most of the stitched borders (though not for March, May, November and December when some of the design falls outside the border.

Then select the 12 squares you want to use for the inner, on-point squares from your layer cake. It might be helpful to lay out the blocks at this point and re-arrange the layer cake squares until you're happy with their order.

The next stage is to cut the windows in these squares to frame your embroidery.

Fold each 10" square in four to find the centre and mark this point.

Take your two cardboard templates (see Material Requirements page 15).

Position each template in turn centrally on the wrong side of the fabric squares and draw around each one. You will now have two concentric circles centred upon the 10" fabric square.

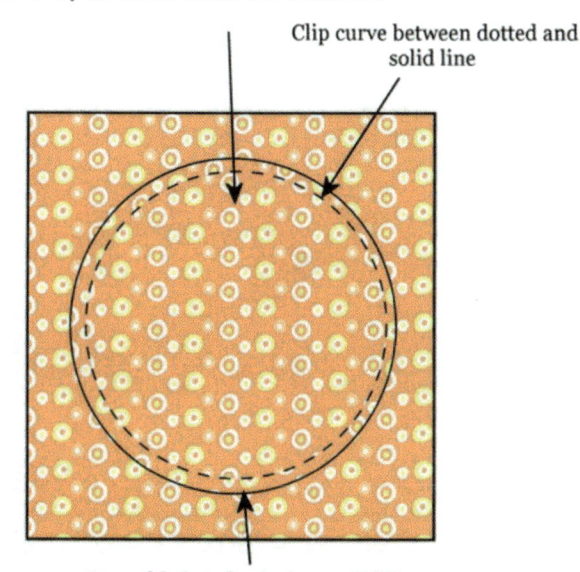

Cut away the fabric within the dotted line

Clip curve between dotted and solid line

Press fabric to back along solid line

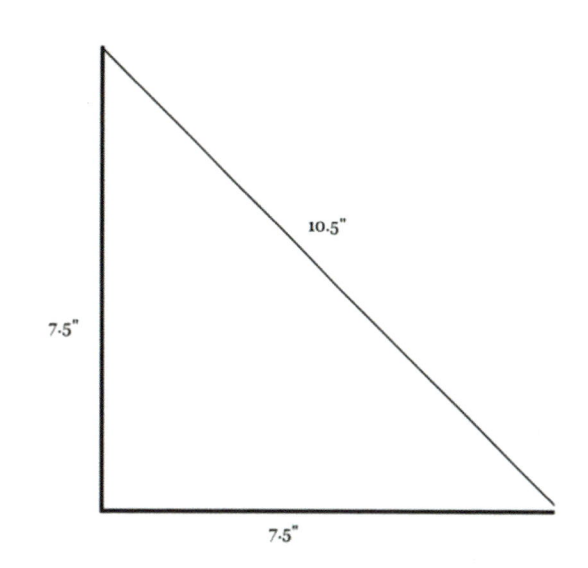

From your biscuit-coloured fabric cut 48 right-angled triangles with one long side of 10 ½" and the two shorter sides measuring 7 ½" each.

When cutting, align the two shorter sides along the grain of the fabric.

Be careful when cutting the longer side as you'll be cutting this on the bias and your fabric may stretch and distort if you're not careful. You will also need to be careful when you're stitching along this side as it will stretch and distort easily.

Cut out the smaller (inner) circle shown by the dotted line in the diagram above.

Clip into the edge to the line you drew for the larger circle.

Turn the edge under on the line and press firmly. This creates the frame for your embroidery.

Position the frame over the embroidery with points of the 10" square at top and bottom so your finished panel will be on point within the quilt. Baste.

Machine top stitch around the edge of the frame ¼" from the edge.

Trim the embroidery fabric to within ½" of stitching on the reverse.

You have now finished piecing your quilt top. Press the whole piece and square if necessary.

Piece your large quilt blocks as shown above. Then, because this quilt features enfolded squares, trim your blocks to 12 ½" square.

This will give you a finished size of 12" with a ¼" seam allowance. If you prefer not to have enfolded squares, then omit this step, but you will then need to adjust all the following dimensions and measurements to allow for the larger size of your basic blocks.

Cut twenty 3 ½" squares from floral fabric. You can use the centres of the circles you cut out to frame your embroidered blocks if you wish, together with additional fabric from your layer cake if using.

Cut thirty-one rectangles of mini polka dot fabric measuring 3 ½" x 12 ½" each.

Assemble your quilt top as shown in the large picture on page 83.

Pay attention to the seams when pressing - either press open or in opposite directions to minimise bulk at the rear.

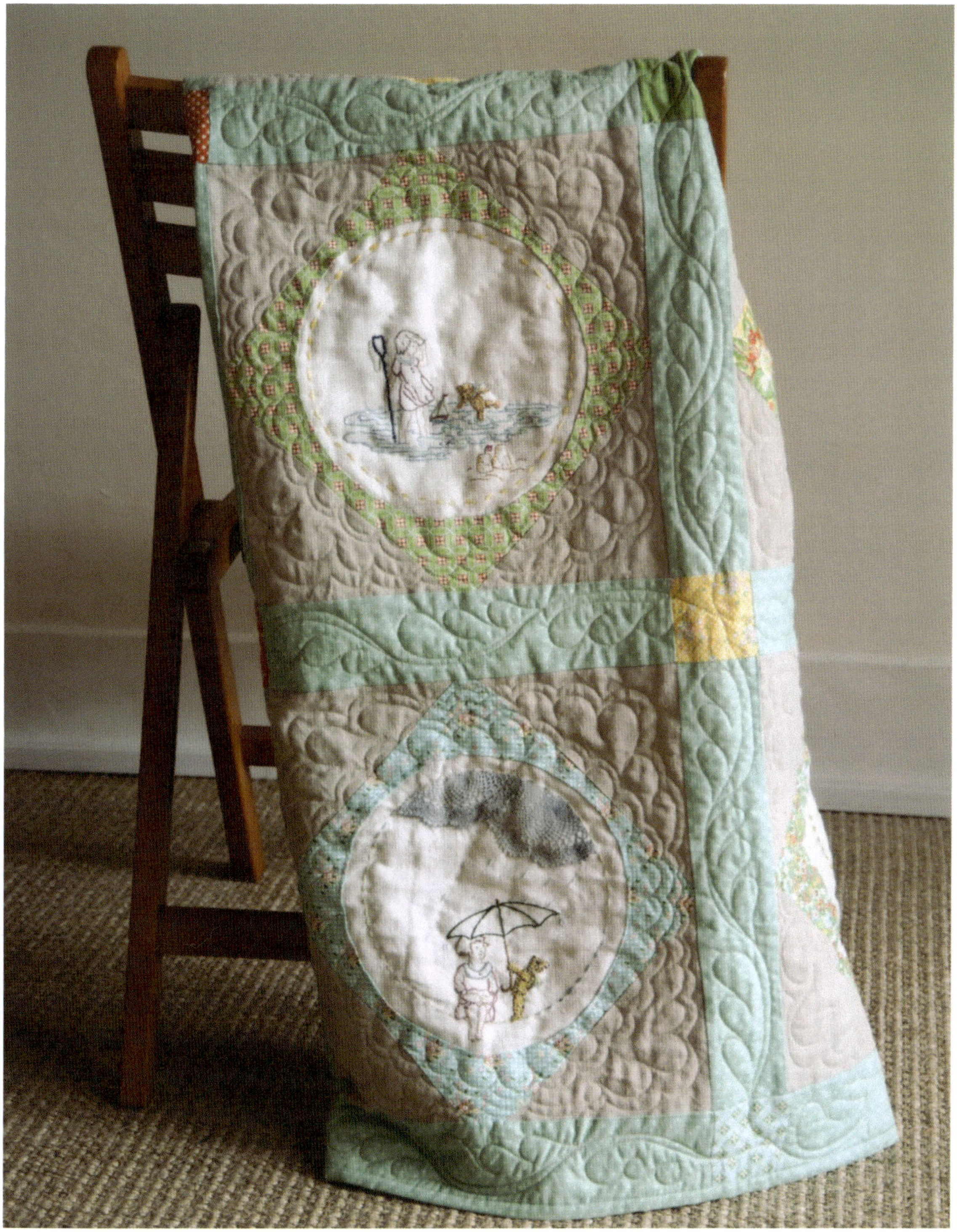

FINISHING YOUR QUILT

Quilting is the name given to the stitching process that secures the three layers of your quilt - the top, batting and backing - together and stops them from sliding around.

There are many ways to quilt your project. The quilt I made (shown in this book) was professionally long-arm quilted with a feather design along the sashing and loops around the central panel.

You may of course prefer to quilt it yourself, either by hand or machine at home.

Whatever method you decide to use, you may need to quilt your embroidered blocks by hand using a hand quilting stitch. This is a small running stitch that penetrates all three layers of your quilt. You can see the hand quilting in the image of the August block above.

When hand-quilting the blocks use thread that is the same colour as the fabric you stitched on as you want it to disappear into the background.

To begin hand quilting, thread your needle with an 18" length of thread, knot it and insert your needle from the front of the quilt into the batting a short distance from where you plan to start. Bring your needle out at your starting point. Then pull lightly on the thread so the knot slips through the top fabric and into the batting.

Note: You should always use a quilting needle for this process, it's short and strong enough to make several stitches through the quilt layers.)

Hand quilting uses a rocking motion of your sewing hand. It's a really good idea to wear a thimble on the first or middle finger of your sewing hand. This hand will stay on top of the quilting whilst your other hand remains below - the index finger of this hand should also be protected.

Push your needle vertically through the layers so the stitches are snug against the top fabric, making slight indentations, and repeat until your quilting is finished.

To secure the end of your thread, tie a knot a short distance from your work, make one last stitch through the batting and the top, then back to the top again a couple of inches away. Finally pull the knot through to the inside of the batting and cut your thread.

Finish your quilt by binding, either with bias strips cut from the backing fabric or purpose-bought binding.

Then add a label to the reverse (see next page for suggested design).

ADDING YOUR LABEL

A well-made quilt is quite likely to outlive the person who stitched it and become an heirloom, passed down through the generations, so it's worth taking just a little time at the end of your project to create a permanent record that your quilt will carry with it as long as it survives.

Anyone who receives, buys, or uses it in the future will thank you for recording the unique facts that make each quilt a bit of living history.

There are many ways of creating your quilt label and you might like to consider incorporating the Rosie & Bear design above:

• Hand write it with permanent ink. Write directly onto the quilt label or even the quilt backing with a fine-tipped, permanent marker. If you write on the backing, test first to make sure it doesn't bleed.

• Embroider by hand or machine. You can also buy custom-made labels embroidered with your information.

• Use a computer and ink jet or all-in-one printer. You can design a custom quilt label using any computer graphics program, including photos, special fonts, or any graphic elements you'd like, then print the label on a pretreated printable fabric sheet. It's also possible to make your own printable fabric sheets and print the label on them.

• Use a vintage linen doily or handkerchief. Write the quilt details on the doily or handkerchief with a permanent fabric marker.

Place the quilt label where it won't show if the quilt is hung up on a wall or laid out on a bed. Many quilters like to put it on the bottom right corner of the quilt's back side. To discourage its removal sew it firmly to the backing fabric before you assemble the quilt, then hand- or machine-quilt right through the label.

GLOSSARY OF STITCHES

BUTTONHOLE OR BLANKET STITCH

Working from left to right, bring your needle out on the bottom line (dotted), insert it above on the top line a little to the right and bring it out again immediately below, drawing the needle through over the working thread. Then insert your needle again on the top line a little further along and repeat the process.

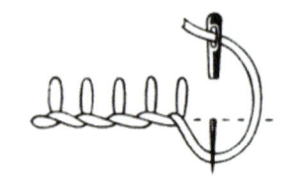

CHAIN STITCH

Bring your thread out at the top of the line you want to cover and hold it down on the material a little to the left with your left thumb. Then re-insert your needle into the exact spot it first emerged and bring it out again a short distance below (according to the length of stitch required). Then draw it through over the loop of working thread as shown in the diagram and repeat.

FRENCH KNOTS

Bring your thread through at the spot you want the knot to be, then hold it down firmly with your left thumb and first finger. Twist your needle two or three times around the held thread (A in the diagram) and then, with the twists pulled nearly tight upon your needle and the thread still held firmly in your left hand, turn the point of the needle around and re-insert into the fabric close to where the thread first emerged (B). Pull your needle and thread through the twists to the back of your fabric or, if you're working your knots in a line, then bring your needle out again at the required spot and repeat.

SATIN STITCH

The stitch simply consists of carrying the thread under the space to be filled and then returning beneath the fabric to the starting point again. It does take practice though, to make the stitches lie evenly and closely together while keeping a neat firm edge to the shape you're filling. Satin stitches can be worked in any direction, and be any length, but the longer they become, the more unwieldy and untidy they appear.

STEM STITCH

This stitch is worked from left to right and your needle should emerge at the end of the line you wish to cover. It then re-enters the fabric a little further along and emerges again a short distance to the left. In effect, your needle is taking a long step forward and a short step back each time.

BUSTLE & SEW

The "Around the Year Quilt Book" is a Bustle & Sew publication. To see my full range of Rosie & Bear embroidery patterns, together with many more stitching, applique, softie and quilting projects please visit my website:

www.bustleandsew.com

Bustle & Sew designs

You can also find out about my Bustle & Sew Magazine on my website. This is my monthly e-zine packed with unique projects, articles, features and loads more, and is by far the best (and nicest!) way to build your collection of Bustle & Sew patterns…

You'll never be stuck for ideas again!! Just visit the magazine page on my website to learn more:

www.bustleandsew.com/magazine.

Printed in Great Britain
by Amazon.co.uk, Ltd.,
Marston Gate.